P9-CDD-704

WAIT,
–
WHAT?

AND LIFE'S OTHER
ESSENTIAL QUESTIONS

–

JAMES E. RYAN

Dean of Harvard's Graduate School of Education

HarperOne

An Imprint of HarperCollins*Publishers*

HarperCollins books may be purchased for educational, business, or sales promotional use. For information, please email the Special Markets Department at SPsales@harpercollins.com.

First HarperOne hardcover published

FIRST EDITION

Designed by Progressive Publishing Services

Library of Congress Cataloging-in-Publication Data is available upon request.

ISBN 978–0–06–266457–0

17 18 19 20 21   LSC   10 9 8

For Doug Kendall

1964–2015

CONTENTS

Why Do You Ask?

In case you are wondering, there are really only five essential questions in life. These are the questions you should ask yourself and others on a regular basis. If you get into the habit of asking these five questions, you will live a happier and more successful life. You will also be in a position, at the end of the day, to give a good answer to what I will call the bonus question—which is probably the most important question you will ever face.

Before you roll your eyes or, worse yet, put down this book, let me say this: I completely get that what I just wrote might seem grandiose and even a bit outlandish. My only excuse is that this book started as a graduation speech, and graduation speeches are meant to be grandiose. And if you think what you just read seems grandiose, you should listen to my speech! In any event, I would ask that you not judge me too harshly—not yet, anyway. I can at least promise that the book is more nuanced, and hopefully funnier, than the speech. It's definitely longer.

I gave the speech in my capacity as dean of the Harvard Graduate School of Education. Each year at graduation, I am obliged to offer a few "brief remarks," which are usually not as brief as they should be. The graduating students and their families, in turn, are obliged to listen—just as countless others across the country are forced to suffer through a slew of banalities and platitudes while fighting off boredom (not to mention heat stroke) in exchange for a diploma. I thought my speech last year about questions was okay. Not great, but okay.

I never expected the speech would go "viral," but viral it went. Millions of people watched a short clip of the speech online. Many offered flattering, generous comments. Some offered disgruntled and downright unflattering comments, most of which I remember, and some of which were very funny. Such is the world of online commentary and my psyche—more on the latter in a bit.

The next thing I knew, an editor emailed to suggest I turn the speech into a book. And the next thing you knew, you were reading it, at least up until this point.

So why a speech and then a book about the importance of asking good questions, especially five essential questions? Good question. (Get it?) The answer is, at least in part, personal.

I have always been fascinated, bordering on obsessed, with questions. Like most kids, I asked a lot of questions when I was younger. The problem, especially for my friends and family, is that I never outgrew that habit. I recall, with some embarrassment, many question-filled dinner conversations with my parents and my poor sister, who had to suffer through a barrage of inquiries and follow-ups.

As I grew older, my questions were less of the "why is the sky blue" sort and more like questions a lawyer might ask when cross-examining a witness, though more persistent than hostile. Or so I liked to think. I would ask my parents why they believed certain things to be true and whether they had any evidence to back up their beliefs. So I asked my mom what proof she had that Ronald Reagan would be a good president, and I asked my dad what proof he had that Reagan would be a lousy president. I asked them both what real evidence they had that the Pope was God's representative on Earth. Not all of the subjects were so lofty. I was just as ready to cross-examine my parents about more mundane topics, like why they thought it was important that I eat brussels sprouts or why anyone would consider liver and onions to be food.

In short, I was annoying. My father, who never attended college, didn't quite know what to make of my constant questions and the fact that asking questions and throwing a ball seemed to be my only real talents. Unlike him, I was not mechanically inclined and could not fix a thing. I had no practical skills at all. But I never ran out of questions, which is why my father repeatedly told me that I had better become a lawyer. He couldn't imagine me earning a living any other way.

I ultimately followed my father's advice, and after graduating from college, I attended law school. It fit me like a glove. Law professors, as you may know, mostly teach by the Socratic method, or at least a modified version of it. They will call on law students and pose question after question, testing whether the answers offered by the students hold up to additional inquiry or a slight change of facts. Done well, this series of questions forces students to think hard about the implications of their arguments and to search for general principles of law that can be applied across a number of different contexts.

I felt like I had found my people, which is one of the reasons why, after practicing law for a few years, I decided to become a law professor.

Shortly after I began as a professor at the University of Virginia Law School, which was also the school I attended as a student, my parents visited me in Charlottesville. My father asked if he could sit in on one of my classes. In retrospect, it was a poignant experience, as it was the only time he would see me teach. He died a few months later, suddenly and unexpectedly, of a heart attack.

My dad was a little surprised that I had chosen to become a law professor. He knew I loved practicing law, and he wasn't entirely convinced that being a professor was a real job. But after witnessing the class, which I spent asking students question after question, my father realized that I had managed to find maybe the one job in the world for which I was naturally well-suited. "This is what you were meant to do," he told me, adding—mostly in jest—that he couldn't believe I was paid to ask students questions that seemed just as annoying as the ones I asked around the dinner table when I was younger.

After teaching law for fifteen years at the University of Virginia, I unexpectedly received an offer to become the dean of Harvard's education school. I had been writing and teaching about education law my entire career, so it was not a completely crazy idea to move to an education school. And I cared deeply about educational opportunity, having benefitted greatly from the education I received in my small hometown in northern New Jersey and, later, at Yale and the University of Virginia.

Like my father, my mother did not attend college, yet they both firmly believed in the power of education, and I experienced that power firsthand. Teachers at my public high school in New Jersey helped me get into Yale as an undergraduate, and that experience changed my life—it opened doors that I didn't even know existed. It also led me to ask a question I have been attempting to answer most of my professional life: Why does our public education system work well for some kids but fail so many others, especially those who are already disadvantaged? I accepted the deanship at Harvard because it seemed like a once-in-a-lifetime chance to work with a dedicated and inspiring group of people, all of whom are intensely committed to improving educational opportunities for students too often neglected.

As I discovered in my first year on the job, deans have to give a lot of speeches. The most important speech is the one at graduation. It is also the most difficult to get right.

I wasn't quite sure what to talk about in my first graduation speech, so I resurrected a speech I gave at my high school graduation. (Yes, I was a little desperate.) The topic of my speech was the highly original one of "time," and in high school the entire speech consisted of disconnected quotations from famous people, plucked from *Bartlett's Familiar Quotations*, about the sanctity of time—so Helen Keller on time, Einstein on time, Yogi Berra on time. When I reworked the speech for the Harvard graduating class of 2014, I realized that what I was trying to say thirty years earlier was that we shouldn't waste time being afraid—of the past, the future, uncertainty, other people, new ideas, or new situations. I still believe that to be true.

My second year, I spoke about another topic that had occupied my attention for a long time: the sin of omission. I grew up in the Catholic Church, attending Mass every week and serving as an altar boy. Catholics, in case you don't already know, are big on sin, and the sin of omission in particular.

I learned about the sin of omission during my first confession. About a year earlier, when I was eleven, my friend and I accidentally set my backyard on fire. We were trying to ignite a leaf with a magnifying glass. When that didn't work, we decided to douse some leaves in gasoline. Turns out that worked really well—so well, in fact, that a fairly large blaze erupted in my backyard. My friend and I eventually managed to put the fire out, but not before I singed both of my eyebrows.

Later that night, when my parents asked if I had any idea why there was a large black patch of burnt grass in our backyard, I pretended to be as surprised as they were.

"That's odd," my dad said.

I asked him why he thought it was odd.

"Because I'm pretty sure you started the day with eyebrows."

He didn't press any further. I'm sure he expected that I would eventually confess, which I did. But I confessed first to a priest, and then, only much later, to my parents.

Initially, I wasn't sure I would admit to this particular sin during my first confession. It seemed like a pretty big one to talk about right out of the gate, and it dawned on me that it was really two sins—lighting the fire, and then, as politicians sometimes say, "misremembering" that I had done so when asked by my parents.

When it came time to give my confession, I first asked the priest what happens if you don't confess all of your sins. I wanted to know my options, basically. "That, too," he said, "would be a sin. A sin of omission." *Damn*, I thought—though obviously didn't say. Failing to do something you ought to do, the priest explained, can be just as much a sin as intentionally doing something wrong.

The idea that you could sin by doing nothing bewildered me at first, but over the years I came to believe that sins of omission are often more harmful—to others and ourselves—than sins of commission. Indeed, I believe they are usually the source of our deepest regrets, which is why I ultimately told my parents about setting the fire in the backyard. It is also why I talked about the sin of omission during my second graduation speech as dean. I suggested that the students should pay close attention to what they are *not* doing.

In spring of 2016, as graduation approached, my friends and colleagues began asking what I planned to talk about in my speech. For a while, I simply replied, reflexively: "That's a good question," which is, I know, a lame answer. But then I realized that, while it might be a bad answer, "good questions" might actually work as a topic for a graduation speech, especially given my lifelong obsession with the subject.

So the importance of asking—and listening for—good questions became the subject of my speech, and it is the topic of this book. The chapters that follow will discuss five essential questions as well as the final bonus question. But before we get to those specific questions, it might be useful to put them in a broader context. So let me make two suggestions about questions in general.

The first suggestion is to spend more time thinking about the right questions to ask.

Many of us spend too much time worrying about having the right answers. Recent graduates may be especially prone to this worry, having just received a diploma testifying to their knowledge—and their families, especially if they helped pay for the diploma, might also expect some answers. For many of us, however, fretting about the right answers persists throughout our lives. It is a common feature of our professional lives, where we don't want to feel incompetent around our colleagues. It also pervades our personal lives, where we don't want to seem clueless to those who might be depending on us. New parents, for example, want to have answers for and about their kids. Just like new employees, new parents tend to get nervous if they come across a question they can't answer, which of course happens very frequently when you are new at anything. This is why new experiences can be stressful. If you think you are supposed to have all of the answers, and all you have are questions, who wouldn't be stressed?

I suffered through this phenomenon when I became a dean. I thought at first that a big part of my job was to have all of the answers. Leaders, after all, are supposed to set forth a vision. Articulating a vision is, in a sense, an answer to the crucial question: What is this institution all about, at the end of the day? I confess I didn't have much of a vision when I began. I barely knew where to find the closest bathroom. Not having answers, much less a vision, made me nervous at first, to the point of despair and occasional panic.

After a while, however, I grew tired of pretending I knew the answers, so I started to ask questions, even in response to questions. As in: "That's a good question. What do you think?" I came to realize that asking good questions is just as important for deans as it is for law professors, though the questions are certainly different. It is only by asking questions of others, for example, that you can articulate a vision that is compelling to those with whom you work. Until I came to that realization, I spent far too much time stressed that I could not immediately answer all of the questions I faced, both large and small.

This is not to say that answers are irrelevant or unimportant. Instead, it is to suggest that questions are just as important as answers, often more so. The simple truth is that an answer can only be as good as the question asked. If you ask the wrong question, you are going to get the wrong answer.

I know this from experience—many experiences, actually, but I will share just one. The scene was a law school dance in Charlottesville, in 1990. I had finally mustered the courage to introduce myself to Katie Homer, a fellow law student on whom I had developed a large crush. But I made two mistakes. First, I decided to introduce myself while Katie was dancing with someone else. (Don't ask me why, though that would be a good question.) The second and more important mistake is that I lost my nerve at the last minute, and instead of introducing myself to Katie, I introduced myself to her dance partner, whom I'll call Norman. I asked, quite loudly so I could be heard over the music: "Are you Norman, by any chance? I ask because I think we're in Civil Procedure class together, and I've really admired your contributions to class discussion." Norman cheerfully answered: "I sure am, and thanks!"

Now, given the question I asked, Norman responded with a perfectly appropriate answer. But it was still the wrong answer. The right answer, to me anyway, would have been: "I'm Katie Homer. It's so nice to meet you, and, yes, I actually would like to marry you." But without asking the right question, I couldn't hope to get the right answer. Luckily for me, Katie understood the real question I was trying to ask, which helps explain why we are married today.

Posing good questions is harder than it might seem. I say this not simply by way of explaining why I asked the wrong question at the dance. Asking good questions is hard because it requires you to see past the easy answers and to focus instead on the difficult, the tricky, the mysterious, the awkward, and sometimes the painful. But I suspect that you and your listeners will be richer for the effort, and that this will be true in both your professional and your personal life.

Asking good questions is crucial to success in just about every imaginable career. Good teachers, for example, appreciate that well-posed questions make knowledge come to life and create the spark that lights the flame of curiosity. And there is no greater gift to bestow on children than the gift of curiosity. Effective leaders, even great ones, accept that they don't have all the answers. But they know how to ask the right questions—questions that force others and themselves to move past old and tired answers, questions that open up possibilities that, before the question, went unseen.

Innovators, in any and every field, understand the wisdom of Jonas Salk, who developed the vaccine for polio: "What people think of as the moment of discovery," Salk observed, "is really the discovery of the question." It takes time to discover the question, but it is time well spent. Einstein, who was a big believer in the importance of asking questions, famously said that if he had an hour to solve a problem, and his life depended on it, he would spend the first fifty-five minutes determining the proper question to ask. You might want to save a little more time for the solution than Einstein, but you get the point.

Asking good questions is just as important in your personal life. Good friends ask great questions, as do good parents. They pose questions that, just in the asking, show how much they know and care about you. They ask questions that make you pause, that make you think, that provoke honesty, and that invite a deeper connection. They ask questions that don't so much demand an answer as prove irresistible. Posing irresistible questions, I believe, is an art worth cultivating.

Indeed, asking good questions is part of what makes us human. Pablo Picasso once said he thought computers were useless because all they could provide were answers. That's slightly extreme, and Picasso rendered his judgment long before the advent of Siri and Google, not to mention Watson.

But if you think about it, Siri, Google, and Watson are remarkable at answering some basic questions, but they are not very good at asking them.

Computers are also pretty lousy at interpreting questions that are poorly posed, which leads to my second suggestion: It's important to listen for good questions. It is a cliché to say that there is no such thing as a bad question. That is actually false, but only partially so. There are plenty of questions that are bad at first glance—as in, "Are you Norman from my civil procedure class?" Whether these questions remain bad, however, often depends on the listener. And the suggestion I want to make is that you, as listeners, can turn most bad questions into good ones, provided that you listen carefully and generously.

To be sure, you will occasionally come across some questions that are beyond repair, but many that seem bad at first glance are actually good questions, or at least innocent ones disguised in awkward clothing. To help you see this, I'd like to give you a short quiz or, as they say in education today, a formative assessment. I will tell two stories, both true, and your task is to identify what's different about them.

Shortly after I arrived on the Yale campus as a college freshman in 1984, I struck up a conversation with a female classmate. It was a lively and easy exchange, and after about twenty minutes, my classmate paused and said, "Can I ask you a question?" And I thought to myself, *This is incredible! She's going to ask me to dinner or a movie. Two days into college, and I'm about to be asked out on a date.*

Now, before I tell you the question she actually asked, I should note that at this point in my life I was roughly five feet, three inches tall—a good six inches shorter than the hulking five-foot, nine-inch frame I occupy today. Perhaps more relevant, puberty was to me still just a hypothetical concept. In short, so to speak, I looked like I was about twelve or thirteen years old. So back to the question. My hoped-for-date said, "Um, I'm not sure how best to ask this, but are you one of those, you know, child prodigies?" Needless to say, we didn't go to dinner. Or a movie.

Contrast that question to one my mother was asked about two months after my awkward child prodigy conversation. I grew up in Midland Park, a blue-collar town in northern New Jersey, which was filled with plumbers, electricians, and landscapers.

It was surrounded by wealthier suburbs, whose homeowners employed the plumbers, electricians, and landscapers from Midland Park. Our grocery store, the A&P, was on the border of Midland Park and a wealthy neighboring town. As my mother was putting groceries in her car one day in the A&P parking lot, a particularly well-coiffed woman came over and asked my mom if she was from Midland Park. After my mom told her that she did indeed live in Midland Park, the woman pointed to the Yale sticker on the rear windshield of my parents' car, and said, "I don't mean to pry, but I'm just so curious: was that Yale sticker on the car when you bought it?"

You see the difference between the two questions, right? The first one was innocent, even (a little) funny, which I ultimately recognized once I hit puberty a few, agonizingly long, months later. The second question was hostile—it wasn't even a question, really. It was an insult.

You will get, if you haven't already, some hostile questions in your life—some from strangers, others from colleagues or supervisors or relatives. The trick is to distinguish the hostile ones from the innocent but clumsy ones. Clumsy questions might really be the questioner's way of seeking to get to know you better, or they could just be the product of anxiety and ignorance, neither of which is morally blameworthy. The only truly bad questions are not really questions at all. They are statements disguised as questions that are meant to be demeaning or designed to trip you up. It's worth being wary of those "questions," but I believe it's also worth remaining open to, and generous toward, all other genuine questions, including the clumsy ones.

To give you a more concrete sense of why I believe in the power—and beauty—of good questions, I want to turn now to the five essential questions. These are the questions that you should always be asking, and listening for, even when they are asked in an awkward way. To be sure, these are not the only important questions you can ever ask others and yourself. What is important will often depend on context. These five questions are instead essential, everyday staples of simple and profound conversations alike, questions that are almost always useful, regardless of context. They are questions that can just as readily help you get through a Monday morning as they can help you figure out what you want to do with your life. They are questions that will help you form new relationships and deepen the ones you already have.

* * * *

When I was in elementary school, our school custodian had a huge key ring hanging from his belt. The keys fascinated me, in part because they seemed to outnumber the doors in our elementary school, or at least the doors that you could see as a student. I wondered what other doors, unseen, the keys might unlock, and what lay behind them. I thought the custodian was the most powerful person in school because he had all the keys. To me, keys signaled power.

Questions are like keys. The right question, asked at the right time, will open a door to something you don't yet know, something you haven't yet realized, or something you haven't even considered—about others and about yourself. What I am suggesting is that the five questions that follow are like five crucial keys on a key ring. While you'll certainly need other keys from time to time, you'll never want to be without these five.

CHAPTER ONE

Wait, What?

The first time I ever asked "Wait, what?" was moments before my son, Will, was born.

Katie and I thought we had the whole labor and delivery thing figured out, even though we were first-time parents. We went to birthing classes; we practiced breathing; we watched videos. When the moment came, and Katie's water broke on the morning of February 25, 1996, we knew we were ready.

We checked into the Lenox Hill hospital in New York City and were taken to a labor and delivery room, which was decorated like a room in a Marriot hotel. Because this was her first time, Katie had no real idea whether she was in active labor or not. She had some mild pains, but the veteran nurses were not impressed. As we walked around the hospital, hoping to speed up the process, with Katie mostly smiling and occasionally wincing, one older nurse told her, in classic New York fashion, "Honey, you know what you need? A real contraction."

The real contractions came about ten hours later. They were hard to miss. The problem was that nothing else seemed to be happening, and after a while, Katie and our soon-to-be-son, Will, started to suffer. The doctor came into the room and said nonchalantly that it was time to take us to a different room. This was not part of the original plan, but we went along without question, ironically enough given the topic of this book.

The other room was actually an operating room, so we went from the cozy confines of our ersatz hotel quarters into a brightly lit, cold, tiled chamber. Waiting for us was a team of technicians and nurses. I stood next to Katie's bed, while the doctor explained very calmly that Will was essentially stuck, likely because he had a very large head, and that they had to get him out right away. The doctor asked if we preferred forceps or a suction cup to aid the delivery. Katie screamed, "Just make it stop!" This was not directly responsive to the question, but I decided it was best not to point that out. I instead replied that I thought the doctor might be in a better position to make the choice, given that this was basically our first time at this. He decided on the suction cup.

The next thing I knew, a man appeared next to me and introduced himself as a doctor. He then explained, very calmly, that he was going to press his forearm on Katie's stomach and squeeze out our baby, "kind of like you might squeeze a pit out of an olive." As he reached across Katie's stomach and grabbed the opposite bed rail for leverage, I distinctly remember thinking that we never went over this particular procedure in birthing class, nor was this "squeeze the pit out of the olive" move ever featured in our birthing videos.

But all I could say was "Wait, what?"

Instead of answering, the doctor pressed down on Katie's stomach. Katie politely explained that this was causing her some mild discomfort—I think her exact words were, "Get off me, or I'll kill you." Moments later, Will acted just like an olive pit and popped out.

I had heard the question "Wait, what?" long before I posed it myself in the delivery room. One of my college roommates, Keith Flavell, asked this question all the time. A lovable and affable Canadian, Keith found many of his roommates, including me, hard to comprehend at times. "Wait, what?" became Keith's almost reflexive response to our conversations, which typically contained assertions ranging from the mildly unbelievable to the ludicrous. Yet, to my knowledge, the question was unique to Keith; it was his signature question.

I have since been told that the question is common among Canadians, but I haven't been able to determine if it was common back in the mid-1980s, when Keith and I were in college. In fact, I have not been able to pinpoint where or when this question first appeared. For all I know, Keith started an international trend.

When Keith and I parted ways after graduation, the question largely disappeared from my life, at least for a while. Katie asked the question occasionally, having picked it up from Keith, but I never heard anyone else ask it. Then our son, Will, appropriately enough given his origins, started asking the question about ten years ago. I noticed his friends also posed the question. And then almost overnight, it seemed that everywhere I went, someone was asking this question. It is now a staple of everyday conversations, especially among those under thirty, though it is certainly not confined to Millennials.

Some traditional grammarians may lament the spread of this particular question, complaining perhaps about the seeming superfluity of "wait." Others might go further and point to it as just more proof of the degradation of the English language and the decline of civilization. But haters are going to hate, as they say, and in this case the skeptics are wrong, because "Wait, what?" is a truly great question. Indeed, this deceptively simple question is essential, if not profound, once you fully appreciate how it can be used.

To begin, "Wait, what?" is remarkably flexible, which might explain some of its popularity. The question can be asked in a variety of ways, depending on what the occasion demands. A plain-spoken "Wait, what?" for example, can simply be a way to ask a person to repeat what she said and to elaborate a bit, because the assertion or suggestion was surprising and slightly hard to believe. An elongated "wait" followed by a short but emphasized "what" is a good way to indicate genuine incredulity. It's a bit like asking, politely, "Did you really just say that?" or "Are you *kidding*?" The reverse formulation, featuring a short "wait" followed by an elongated "what" can be used when someone has asked you to do something, and it can effectively convey suspicion and skepticism about the motives behind the request or downright opposition to what is being asked of you.

The last formulation is the way my kids most often pose the question in our conversations. Typically, they ask this question when I get to the point in a conversation where I'm suggesting that they do a chore or two. From their perspective, they hear me saying something like, "Blah, blah, blah, and then I'd like you to clean your room." And at that precise moment, the question inevitably comes: "Wait, whaaat? Did you say clean? Our rooms?"

"Wait, what?" is first on my list of essential questions because it is an effective way of asking for clarification, and clarification is the first step toward truly understanding something—whether it is an idea, an opinion, a belief, or a business proposal. (It's probably not a good idea to ask this question in response to a marriage proposal. Just saying.)

The "wait" that precedes the "what" could be seen as just a useless rhetorical tic. But I think it's crucial because it reminds you (and others) to slow down to make sure you truly understand. Too often we fail to pause for clarification, thinking that we understand something before we do. In doing so, we miss the opportunity to grasp the full significance of an idea, an assertion, or an event. Asking "Wait, what?" is a good way to capture, rather than miss, those opportunities.

To give an example, years ago Katie and I, along with a couple of friends, traveled to Norway to hike and kayak. While there, we met up with another old friend who was working as a bush pilot, taking passengers on sightseeing trips and to remote camping areas. When he heard we were planning to hike near a particular fjord the next day, he asked if we could take one of his clients with us, a nineteen-year old Japanese guy, who wanted to see this particular fjord. We agreed and picked him up the next day.

His English was a little spotty and our Japanese was nonexistent, so it was a fairly quiet ride. When we arrived at the fjord, our new friend immediately jumped out of the car and took an album cover out of his backpack. He then began running around to different spots, stopping occasionally to hold up the album cover and look up the fjord to a large mountain in the distance. Then he would scramble to a different spot and pause again. We all glanced at each other while watching him, not sure what was happening and worried that something might be wrong.

When we finally caught up with him, we saw that the album cover had a picture of a fjord on it, with a large mountain in the distance. The album was a symphony by Edvard Grieg, the Norwegian composer. We finally realized that the picture on the album cover was of the exact place we were visiting, and our new friend was trying to find the precise spot where the picture was taken. He then explained that he had been dreaming his whole life of coming to this spot, and that this was the reason he had spent his life savings to come to Norway.

And that's when Katie asked, "Wait, what?" We eventually learned that this young man grew up in a tiny apartment in Tokyo and had a hard childhood. His one escape was to listen to the Grieg symphony and to dream about one day visiting the place pictured on the cover of the album. To him, it was the most beautiful place in the world. It took a while for us to understand his story, but by asking "Wait, what?" Katie was inviting him to explain and signaling that we wanted to hear his tale, which turned out to be a remarkable one.

Asking "Wait, what?" is also a good way to avoid jumping to conclusions or making snap judgments. Too often we decide very early whether we agree or disagree with someone or with an idea, without making an effort to truly understand the person or the point. Our public conversations, and especially conversations on social media, often seem like exercises in picking sides and choosing teams. We hear or read something, make a quick call, then dismiss those with whom we disagree as ignorant or evil. If we took more time to understand ideas and perspectives, especially new and challenging ones, we might be less dismissive and instead more curious. Even if a better understanding of an idea or perspective doesn't change your mind, it is likely to make you respect or at least appreciate the person proposing the idea more than you would otherwise.

If nothing else, truly understanding an idea or argument enables you to make an informed judgment about it. I learned this by watching U.S. Supreme Court Justice John Paul Stevens, who was one of the best questioners I have ever seen in my professional life. I saw Justice Stevens in action when I clerked for Chief Justice Rehnquist. Clerking was a dream job for a young lawyer, especially one obsessed with questions, in part because we were allowed to attend all of the oral arguments. Each argument lasted an hour, with thirty minutes given to each side. Aside from Justice Thomas, who is legendary for almost never asking a question, the justices peppered the lawyers with questions. Often, the justices made arguments through the lawyers, communicating more to their colleagues on the bench than to the lawyer arguing before the court.

That was not Justice Stevens' style. Although he never uttered the exact question "Wait, what?" this was essentially the question he asked lawyers, time and again. Using various formulations of the same question, he would ask lawyers to clarify a key point of their arguments. He did it in a very respectful, almost gentle way. He was not at all bombastic or intentionally sarcastic, the way some of his colleagues were, Justice Scalia in particular. Instead, he would always begin by saying something like, "Counselor, I'm sorry to interrupt, but I wonder if I could ask you to clarify a point."

Almost without fail, the question that followed hit on the weakest part of the lawyer's case. By requiring the lawyer to slow down her argument and explain the key point—it could be a fact or a point of law—Justice Stevens usually made clear that there was a problem with the lawyer's argument, often a fairly big problem. More than any of his colleagues, Justice Stevens tended to break open the case by asking lawyers *the* question at the center of their case, one they had to answer successfully in order to prevail. If they were unable to answer the question, Justice Stevens could then explain through subsequent questions and in his opinions why their side should lose the case. By asking for clarification first, Justice Stevens put himself in a position to be a strong advocate for the result he thought was demanded in a case.

Justice Stevens' approach to questions illustrates an enduring point: In almost every instance, it is better to ask clarifying questions first and to argue second. Before you advocate for a position, be sure to ask "Wait, what?" Inquiry, in other words, should always precede advocacy.

Of course, this is easier said than done, a fact brought home to me and others who had the good fortune to participate in a master class taught last year by Rakesh Khurana. Rakesh is a professor at the Harvard Business School and is currently serving as the dean of Harvard College. To highlight good teaching around the university, my colleagues and I each year invite talented professors from all across Harvard to offer several master classes at the Graduate School of Education. These professors teach a class, then explain afterward what they were trying to accomplish and why. Rakesh's class highlighted his brilliance at teaching by the case method, which is the way classes are typically taught in business school.

For his master class, Rakesh presented a case to all of us, based on a true story, that involved Jenny, Lee, and Piet. Jenny was a young associate at a small public relations firm, and she was trying to close a deal with a potential client, a Dutch man named Piet. Jenny invited Lee, her mentor and the firm's owner, to an important lunch with Piet. Lee had not yet met Piet. At the lunch, Piet mentioned several times how wonderful it was to be working with Jenny, whom he repeatedly described as an especially attractive young woman. Lee ignored these comments, as did Jenny, and both tried to keep the conversation focused on business. Piet asked if Jenny would be working on the project personally, and Lee offered that she would, along with others from the firm. As the lunch ended, Piet gestured toward Jenny and told Lee that he enjoyed the lunch, as he always loved the chance to have lunch with a pretty girl.

The ensuing discussion in the master class revolved first around Jenny's dilemma and how she should have resolved it. Should she have pointed out that Piet's comments were sexist, which would have risked losing the client? Or should she have remained quiet in order to land the business? The discussion also focused a great deal on Lee and what role Lee should have played. The audience—just like you at this point, I would guess—had a lot to say about Lee, not much of it positive. Many argued that "he" should have stuck up for his young protégé, Jenny, and not let her hang out to dry.

At that point, Rakesh said, feigning that he forgot this detail, "Oh, I'm sorry! I forgot to tell you that Lee is a woman." He paused while that important fact, which no one had sought to clarify, sunk in. The audience, myself included, immediately gasped and said, "Wait, what?" We then laughed sheepishly as we realized that we had been making all sorts of arguments about Lee's behavior based on our shared assumption that Lee was a man—even though the case we had read never specified Lee's gender.

And that was basically Rakesh's point. We assumed we were justified in condemning Lee. Rakesh, however, taught us not to be so sure, and he demonstrated how prone we are to make arguments and judgments based on false assumptions. You might still criticize Lee's behavior, but it is obviously better to do that once you possess all of the facts. It is a point I will not soon forget and one I believe worth remembering.

It is especially worth remembering in difficult situations, whether at home or at work. When faced with difficult conversations or emotionally charged situations, it is always a challenge to pause to ask if you have all of the facts you need to draw fair conclusions. It is easy—too easy—simply to react, often passionately and often based on assumptions rather than facts. Reminding yourself to ask "Wait, what?" is a way to guard against jumping too quickly to conclusions.

Asking "Wait, what?" not only helps clarify your own thinking, it can also help others do the same. For this reason, I have found it is useful as a parent to turn the table on my kids and pose the "Wait, what?" question to them. For the parents reading this book, you know that your kids can sometimes engage in what we might charitably call faulty reasoning. They might underestimate the risks or costs involved in an unsupervised adventure with friends. They might underestimate the amount of time it will take to complete a task. More seriously, they might, because of insecurity, misjudge their own place in the world and fail to see their strengths or attractiveness to others.

Adults are prone to the same mistakes. Those who lack confidence, for example, routinely make all sorts of faulty assumptions and poor inferences, assuming that they lack the competence, charisma, or talent to succeed in their careers or relationships. When your kids, friends, or other family members underestimate themselves, asking them a version of "Wait, what?" can help reveal those faulty assumptions and inferences, which can then be the primary focus of the conversation. Indeed, you can then follow up with a version of the second essential question—"I wonder why you believe that about yourself?"—to encourage your friends or relatives to reassess their thinking. These conversations are not always easy, but they are as essential as the questions that encourage them.

A quick word, finally, about being a good listener. It is useful as a listener to be on the lookout for versions of the "Wait, what?" question. Some things you say will inevitably provoke opposition or challenge from friends, family members, or colleagues. It is easy, when on the receiving end of these challenges, to immediately begin an argument, trying to defend your position. But you might try to remember that the person posing the challenge or expressing opposition could simply be in need of further explanation or may just need to better understand the rationale or motivation behind what you are saying.

Approaching questions this way is essentially the flip side of asking questions of others before you begin an argument with them. The key is to not let yourself get drawn into a possibly needless argument before you have fully explained your own thinking. So the next time someone says in response to a suggestion or proposal, "That's ridiculous," or, "That seems like a totally dumb idea," remind yourself that they might simply be asking, "Wait, what?" They might be asking for a deeper explanation. They may still disagree with you, but after hearing your explanation in full, they will unlikely think your idea is ridiculous or dumb.

In short, "Wait, what?" is an essential question because it is at the heart of understanding, which in turn is crucial to a fulfilling and rewarding life, both professionally and personally. The world will be a richer place for you the more you understand the people and ideas you encounter in it. Cultivating the habit of understanding first and making judgments second will also help you avoid pointless conflicts and create deeper connections with those around you. That's not a bad result from a seemingly simple question.

CHAPTER TWO

I Wonder ...?

Conventional wisdom suggests that curiosity can be dangerous, especially to cats. But in my experience, the opposite is true.

Shortly after we were married, Katie and I lived briefly in the Netherlands, which is famously filled with canals. I like to run, and one morning I ran through a grassy field in a park a few miles from our apartment. I noticed that the grass ahead was lime green, while the grass I was running over was dark green. Instead of asking, "I wonder why the grass changes color up ahead," I charged ahead.

It was only when I was hurtling over the side of a canal that I realized that the lime green "grass" was actually algae. But by that point it was too late. The next thing I knew, I was waist deep in the canal, covered in green slime, checking for injuries and looking around to see if anyone had noticed. I pulled myself out of the canal, nothing injured but my pride, as several witnesses called out some words in Dutch, which roughly translated to, "That was hilarious. You ran straight into the canal!" I then had to run several miles to get home, all the while looking like Sigmund the Sea Monster, the star of a great 1970s Saturday-morning television show.

Which leads me to the second essential question: "I wonder . . . ?" Before you object, I recognize that this is, technically, not a complete question. It is instead the first half of a series of questions. "I wonder" can be paired, at the very least, with both "why" and "if." This chapter is about these two variations on a single theme, namely the questions "I wonder why?" and "I wonder if?"

Asking "I wonder why?" allows you to remain curious about the world, which would have come in handy on my run in the Netherlands. Asking "I wonder if?" allows you to remain engaged with the world and is a way to prompt yourself to try something new. It is also the way to begin thinking about how you might improve the world, or at least your corner of it. Though distinct, these questions are also related. It is hard to ask "I wonder why?" for example, without also eventually asking, "I wonder if?" If this all seems a little mysterious, stay tuned.

Albert Einstein, in a classic humble brag, once remarked: "I have no special talents. I am only passionately curious." The first half of that statement was surely false, while the second half was undoubtedly true. Einstein was passionately curious about the world around him, both seen and unseen. "The important thing," he observed, "is to not stop questioning. Never lose a holy curiosity."

Curiosity begins with asking "I wonder why?" When children first encounter the world, this is the question foremost on their minds. "Why?" is their go-to question and makes up an inordinate part of their daily conversations. For whatever reason, most people, I have noticed, tend to become less curious about the world as they age. It may be that their curiosity was not sufficiently encouraged by parents or teachers, who can become weary of the "why" question. The logistics of life can also crowd out curiosity, as simply getting through the day presents its own challenges for adults. Regardless of the reason, it is the exceptional adult who has retained a child's innate curiosity about the world around her.

If you commit to asking "I wonder why?" you can prod yourself to remain curious. Even if others get tired of hearing it or cannot answer the question, you should never stop posing it to yourself. I don't mean that you should give up your job or spend all of your time daydreaming. I am only suggesting that you take the time to look around you—whether at the people near you or your physical surroundings—and remember to ask "I wonder why?"

This single question is the key that can unlock a wealth of stories and solve a host of mysteries, large and small. This is the question that launches discoveries and leads to remarkable insights. It is the question that scientists, from Marie Curie to Stephen Hawking, have asked about the world around them. It is the question great artists and writers have asked for centuries. To scientists and artists, not to mention great teachers and entrepreneurs, the world is filled with puzzles waiting to be solved.

You do not need to be a world-class scientist or artist to appreciate that the world contains mysteries and puzzles, or even to solve some of them. You just need to look around and ask questions. Too often, we see the world as static, failing to appreciate that what we see in front of us is the product of the past—of forces no longer visible. All around us are messages and clues waiting to be discovered and interpreted.

Take something as simple as a rock wall marking a field. If you have traveled in rural areas, especially in New England, you will undoubtedly have seen a rock wall. Some line the land where I live in Massachusetts; some extend through the woods behind my house. These silent markers are so ubiquitous that they are easy to overlook. Indeed, I thought little of them until my daughter, Phebe, who was eight years old at the time, asked me why there were so many rock walls where we lived.

After saying "Beats me," I decided to investigate a bit. The walls, it turns out, are far more interesting than they might appear. The rocks came to the surface thousands of years ago when glaciers churned up pieces of granite and limestone. (Okay, that part's pretty boring, but it gets better.) In the colonial and revolutionary periods, farmers came across these rocks when clearing their fields. At first they piled the rocks haphazardly, but later they used them to build walls establishing their property lines. As families in the Northeast shifted their attention away from agriculture toward industry, the walls were ignored. Many became overgrown during the Industrial

Revolution. Only later, in the mid-twentieth century, were the walls rediscovered and rightly celebrated, both for their connection to our earliest history as a nation and because of the thought, care, and labor that went into building them.

To see these walls—to truly see them—you have to ask, like Phebe did: I wonder why there are so many rock walls? That inevitably leads to other questions: I wonder how old they are? I wonder why (and how) they were built? I wonder why some are running through the woods, why some are falling apart, why some are pristine? Once you start asking and answering these questions, what was once mundane becomes mysterious and then fascinating.

My own search ultimately led me to Henry David Thoreau, who marveled at the stone walls near Walden Pond in Concord, which is not far from my home. Writing in his journal in 1850, Thoreau observed: "We are never prepared to believe that our ancestors lifted large stones or built thick walls. How can their work be so visible and permanent and themselves so transient? When I see a stone which it must have taken many yoke of oxen to move, lying in a bank wall . . . I am curiously surprised, because it suggests an energy and force of which we have no memorials." What started as largely invisible walls turned into a local history lesson and a set of existential questions from Thoreau, all of which made Phebe and me feel more connected to the world around us and all of which started with asking "I wonder why?"

A wall in a field is just a simple example, but everywhere you look—if you really take the time to look—there are stories. Streets, buildings, stars, trees, trains, boats, animals—all of them have a past and a story to tell. This is especially true of the people around you, whether they are sitting next to you in a lecture hall or in the next cubicle. Everyone has a unique story. To hear these stories, and to understand the world around you, from the beliefs and values of a community to the experiences of the people in it, you simply have to take the time to notice and to ask "I wonder why?"

Learning these stories will inevitably enrich your life. It might even lengthen it. Curiosity, it turns out, is conducive to health and happiness, as scores of social scientists have documented. Curious people, not surprisingly, are likely to learn more and to retain more of what they learn. Curious people are likely to be more attractive to others, as people are attracted to those who seem interested in them. Curiosity also leads to empathy, an emotion that seems in short supply today. Curious people are likely to be healthier, and to experience less anxiety in particular, because they see new situations as an opportunity to learn rather than an opportunity to realize that they don't know enough. Curious people are also, according to some studies, likely to live longer, presumably because they are more engaged with the world around them.

Just as asking "I wonder why?" will keep you curious about the world, asking "I wonder if?" will keep you engaged in the world. Nearly every adventure I have been on, and nearly every new thing I have tried, began with the question: "I wonder if I could do that?" The answers have not been uniform.

I wondered if I could row crew in college (no; I was too short, as you might remember); I wondered if I could join an a cappella group (no, because it turns out you need to be able to sing); I wondered if I could play rugby instead (yes, as height and singing ability don't matter much); I wondered if I could support myself for six months after college, in Australia, by working as a garbage collector (not really; once I found a dead cat in a garbage can, I was done); I wondered if I could bungee jump (yes, but never again); I wondered if I could learn to play ice hockey as an adult (not well, according to my kids and my teammates); I wondered if I could learn how to juggle (yes, because it's actually not that hard); I wondered, five years ago, if I could learn to surf (sort of, is the answer my kids would give); and I wondered if I could learn to play the piano (no, unless "Mary Had a Little Lamb" counts; it doesn't if you ask Katie). As this list suggests, not all new things you try will succeed, which is just what you would expect. But if you never stop asking "I wonder if I could do that," you are bound to find things you love to do.

While the question "I wonder if?" is a question worth asking on its own, it is also closely connected to the question "I wonder why?" Once you start asking "I wonder why?" and especially if you get an unsatisfying answer, you are inevitably going to ask "I wonder if things could be different?" Put another way, to ask "I wonder why?" about the present naturally raises the question "I wonder if?" about the future.

Take a social problem such as school segregation, a topic I studied as a law professor. From one perspective, school segregation can seem like a thing of the past. If we define school segregation as a system where students are compelled by law to attend one school or another based on race, that system is dead. It was struck down as unconstitutional in *Brown v. Board of Education,* decided in 1954. Yet legally compelled segregation is only one form of school segregation. There is another form, sometimes called de facto segregation, the legal term for segregation "in fact," meaning segregation that does not arise because of laws compelling it, but is instead caused by a range of other factors. This type of segregation continues to exist.

Indeed, over the last twenty years or so, de facto segregation has continued to grow. Our schools are becoming more segregated by race and socioeconomic status, not less. The obvious question is why? Thankfully, a number of outstanding advocates and scholars have been asking this question, and the answers they have discovered are fairly straightforward. Desegregation decrees, which were always meant to be temporary, are being lifted by courts, so programs to integrate schools are being dismantled; neighborhoods remain segregated, so neighborhood schools remain segregated; and charter schools tend to focus on serving poor students of color, not on creating integrated schools.

Once these advocates began asking and answering the question "I wonder why?" they inevitably began asking "I wonder if?" I wonder if we could create more integrated neighborhoods? I wonder if we could offer students options to attend schools out of their segregated neighborhoods? I wonder if at least some charter schools could focus on diversity as part of their mission? And through those questions, these advocates have brought renewed attention to segregation, so much so that they captured the imagination of U.S. Secretary of Education John King, who made school integration and diversity a key part of his agenda.

This does not mean, of course, that change will be automatic. There is a long way to go before integrated schools become the rule rather than the exception. But without these individuals asking "I wonder why?" and "I wonder if?" and refusing to accept the status quo as inevitable, it is unlikely that Secretary King would have made school integration a priority for the federal government.

The lesson I draw from this example, as well as others, is that even the most stubborn facts of life surrounding you are worth questioning. Sometimes, the most grave injustices and inequities seem so intractable that asking why they persist seems pointless. Some feel this way, for example, about school segregation. But most of what you see around you is not impervious to change or improvement. And the very first step toward altering what you see is to ask "I wonder why?" and then to follow that question with another: "I wonder if?"

These two related questions are just as useful to ask in your personal life as they are in your professional life. I know this from one experience in particular, which can serve both as a cautionary tale and as confirmation of the importance of asking "I wonder . . . ?"

I first met my biological mother at a rest stop on the Garden State Parkway in New Jersey. I was forty-six years old at the time. I always knew I was adopted. I can no more remember when I learned this fact than I can remember when I learned my name is Jim, or Jimbo, as I was called as a kid. I never recall feeling resentful toward my birth mother or abandoned, in part because my parents made it seem special that I was adopted.

It also didn't hurt that I had a happy childhood. My parents weren't perfect, but they were pretty close or at least seemed so to me. We didn't have much money, but I had all I thought necessary for a good childhood—a bicycle, baseball mitt, cleats, sneakers, friends in my neighborhood, one week a year at the Jersey Shore, two parents whose lives revolved around their family, and a sister who put up with me most of the time.

Perhaps because of all of this, I was also never that curious about my biological parents. I was adopted through a Catholic adoption agency in a completely closed process. What little I knew was from a story my mother sometimes told, about how she and my dad got a call one day that a baby was "ready" for them, and that they should come to a hospital in Elizabeth, New Jersey, in two days. When a nun brought me into the room where my parents were waiting, I was wearing a hand-knit sweater and a necklace with a medallion of St. Christopher, the patron saint of travelers. My mom asked the nun where the sweater and medallion had come from, and the nun teared up—as did my mother at this point in the story—and said: "I can't tell you. I can only say they come from someone who loves him very much."

You might have thought that story would pique my curiosity, but it didn't. Mostly, it reinforced a vague feeling of gratitude. I figured that it had to have been hard to give up a baby for adoption, and I was grateful for the sacrifice. But I wasn't that interested in knowing more about my biological parents because I already had what seemed to me a complete family.

I also figured I knew the story. I imagined that my biological parents were teenagers, maybe high school sweethearts, who decided they were too young to raise a child. So I figured my biological mother carried me to term, put me up for adoption, and then went on with her life. That is a classic story behind adoption, and I just assumed I fit the mold. So I never really asked "I wonder why" I was adopted, nor did I ask "I wonder if" I could ever find my biological parents, even though my (adoptive) parents always said they would try to help me if I were ever interested in tracking down my birth family.[1]

---

[1] Forgive the footnote here, but just to avoid confusion, I should make clear that if I refer to my parents or my mother or father, without any qualifier, I am referring to my adoptive parents. I will use the qualifier "adoptive" only when it's not clear from the sentence or paragraph whom I am talking about.

Fast forward to 2012. By this point, both of my parents had passed away, each at far too young an age. Katie and I had a family of our own. With the birth of each of our four kids, I grew a little more curious about my biological parents, as none of our kids looked exactly like Katie or me. I wondered if maybe they were the spitting image of some unknown blood relative. But, in the chaos of a full household, those thoughts were fleeting.

Then one day, several years ago, I went on a run with a good friend, who was born in Korea but left with his mother and brother when he was seven. He was trying to track down his father and suggested I try to find my biological parents. I explained my lack of interest, but he persisted. To appease him, I agreed to take a look.

When I returned home from the run, I went online and, within an hour, discovered that adoption agencies in New Jersey will release "non-identifying information" about the adoption, which means they will share everything they know except last names. I tracked down the branch in New Jersey that handled my adoption, emailed them to confirm this was their policy and that they still had my records. "Yep, right here in our files," came the reply. *Who knew it was this easy*, I thought, as I sent off a check to get my report.

Two months later a three-page letter arrived in the mail, detailing my family history and the circumstances of my adoption, which had been culled from reports in my file. The story was not at all what I expected. The letter gave the first names of my birth parents, a family history of their parents and siblings, and a detailed rendition of the circumstances surrounding my adoption. The letter read like the outline for a novel about Irish immigrants, set in the late nineteenth century.

My birth mother, whom I will call Geraldine, was born and raised in Ireland. When she was an adult, she followed her brother to the United States, where she found work with a wealthy family in New York City. She met and fell in love with an Irish bartender (explains a lot, Katie would say later). When Geraldine told my biological father she was pregnant, he confessed that he was married, with three children. Because he was Catholic, he told her, he couldn't consider divorce. (Apparently he could consider adultery. Just saying.) Geraldine broke off all ties with him and traveled across the river to Elizabeth, New Jersey, to a home for unwed mothers-to-be.

Geraldine spent her days knitting (the sweater!) and talking with the nuns about how she might be able to keep me. "She cried every time adoption was brought up," the letter reported. But Geraldine ultimately concluded that she couldn't afford to raise a baby on her own, and she also thought I needed a father. She stayed with me for nine days in the hospital, right up to my adoption. The last line of the letter read, "She left the hospital broken-hearted."

I was stunned. This letter answered questions I had never even thought to ask—like, did I have a name during the first nine days of my life? (It turns out I did; I was named Michael Joseph, after my maternal grandfather.) I handed the letter to Katie, who started crying as she read it. She looked at me after she read the last lines and said, "You need to find Geraldine. You need to tell her everything turned out okay."

Two days later, I received a call from the woman at the adoption agency—I'll call her Barb. Barb had put together the letter based on the records in my file. "Jim," she said in a pitch-perfect New Jersey accent, "I've been doin' this for twenty-five years. Jim, I gotta tell you, I've never come across a story like this. It touched my heart, Jim. You hear what I'm sayin' to you? It really touched my heart." She went on to say she couldn't tell me to try to find Geraldine, because that would cost more money. "But Jim," she said, "I bet she's been wonderin' about you, right?"

That was another thought, I'm embarrassed to say, that hadn't really occurred to me—that my birth mother might be wondering about me.

I sent in another check and waited. Barb and I considered that my birth mother might have returned to Ireland. We also recognized that she might have passed away. Months went by, and I heard nothing. In the meantime, I was contacted out of the blue about becoming the dean at the Harvard Education School. That process preoccupied me and culminated in a call at five o'clock on a Thursday evening in June 2013 from Drew Faust, the president of Harvard University. She was calling to offer me the job.

My head was spinning as I contemplated uprooting my family from Virginia and moving to Massachusetts. It nearly exploded the next morning when the phone rang. It was Barb. "Jim," she said, "Jim. Are you sittin' down?"

"No," I told her.

"Sit down," she said. "We found her." Because I had been thinking about the call with President Faust the night before, for a split second I thought Barb was going to tell me: "Jim, your mother is Drew Faust." But that's not what she said. Instead, she described how they found Geraldine and how she reacted to the news. When contacted by Barb, who said a "relative" was trying to find her, Geraldine and her husband drove to the adoption agency's office in Elizabeth. Geraldine cried when told I had been found and explained to Barb that she had prayed for me every day of my life. "And do you know what her prayer was?" Barb asked me. "She prayed, every day, that the two of you would meet in heaven."

Turns out Geraldine hadn't returned to Ireland after all. She had met and married a wonderful man I will call Joe, had four more kids, and moved to New Jersey. She and her family lived fifteen minutes away from where I grew up! Her kids went to Catholic schools that friends of mine attended. Our paths probably crossed at some point during my childhood.

A few days later, Geraldine and I talked by phone. I first talked to her husband, and before he could say a word, I blurted out something like: "I'm not crazy. I'm not looking for money. I'm not emotionally needy. At least not usually. I just wanted to say thanks and to let Geraldine know that everything turned out okay, and that I'm happy." I could hear him smiling on the other end of the phone, and all he said was that "she's been waiting a long time for this, Jim. And she is the most amazing woman I've ever known." When Geraldine and I finally spoke, the conversation was both surreal and completely natural. She still has an Irish brogue. She asked about Katie and our kids. Then she asked about me, tentatively. We agreed to talk more and, eventually, to meet.

For convenience, we picked a rest stop on the Garden State Parkway because, well, that's where people from New Jersey would think to meet. That morning, my family and I left our home in Virginia for the last time, the only home our kids had known, on our way to a new home in Massachusetts. Our kids were distraught about the move. They hadn't really paid much attention to the Geraldine affair, in part because they were preoccupied with moving and in part because they adored my mother—their grandmother—who had passed away a few years earlier. But when they saw Geraldine, they stopped on a dime and looked back and forth between her and me.

Geraldine is barely five feet tall, spry, and looks like me in a wig. Our likeness is unmistakable and uncanny. In an instant, my kids knew that they were implicated in this whole experience, because they could see a part of themselves in this otherwise total stranger sitting in the rest stop food court, just outside of the Dunkin' Donuts. We sat for two hours talking, looking at pictures, and holding hands. As we left, Geraldine handed my kids envelopes with their names on them. Each card in the envelope contained a $20 bill, which Geraldine suggested they use as ice cream money for the summer.

I eventually met my four half brothers and sisters, one of whom could be my twin, and I talk with Geraldine every couple of weeks. It's a completely and surprisingly uncomplicated relationship, and Geraldine is not shy about suggesting I might call more often. She is impossible not to like. She is quick to smile and laugh, and she is gentle and unfailingly caring. She is familiar and close without being possessive.

If I had never bothered to ask "I wonder why I was adopted?" and then ask "I wonder if I could find my biological mother?" I would never have met Geraldine and her family. To say that my life is richer because I did ask those questions is an understatement. To think that I believed I already knew Geraldine's story was, in retrospect, ridiculous. Just how wrong I was came home to me the day Geraldine introduced me to her other children, all of whom are about my age. We walked into her daughter's house, and Geraldine reached for my hand and didn't let go until I had met all of her other children. Then she turned and gently, without asking or hesitating, fixed my collar. And I realized: Even though she would never be my "mother," in the sense that no one could ever displace my adoptive mom, to Geraldine I have always been and always would be her son.

This is not a story about changing the world, of course, but it did change *my* world, in a remarkable and meaningful way. And this leads to the final point about asking "I wonder why?" and "I wonder if?" These are questions that are useful to ask not simply about the world around you, but to ask yourself. I am not trying to peddle a self-help program here or to endorse navel-gazing, but I believe it's healthy and productive to remain curious about yourself. Why do you have certain habits? Why do you like certain places, foods, events, and people, and what if there are others you would like just as much, if you gave them a chance? Why do new experiences make you nervous? Why are you quiet in meetings or shy at parties? Why are you easily distracted? Why do you sometimes lose your patience with certain members of your family? And what if you tried to change those things about yourself that you would really like to change? Or, just as importantly, what if you just accepted some of those things as part of who you are?

In sum, the question "I wonder why?" is essential because it is at the heart of curiosity, and asking this question is the way to remain interested in the world around you, including your place in it. Asking "I wonder if?" is equally essential because it is the way to remain engaged with the world and to begin thinking about ways to improve your corner of it. If you fail to ask these questions, you risk missing out on joys and possibilities that you don't even realize exist and, as with Geraldine, are sometimes closer than you could ever imagine.

CHAPTER THREE

Couldn't We at Least ...?

The third essential question led to my fourth (equally essential) child, Phebe. I realize that might seem hard to believe, but it's true.

Katie and I planned to have three kids, but then Katie changed her mind. After our third son, Ben, was born, Katie began saying that our family didn't seem complete. Each time she said this, over the course of an entire year, I honestly thought she was joking. To a neutral observer who witnessed our three boys, the notion that our family was incomplete would not have immediately sprung to mind.

A year later, as she continued making this observation, I finally realized she wasn't joking. I asked if it was because we only had boys, and she wanted a girl. I knew she was hoping to use the name Phebe, an unusual spelling of Phoebe that extends back in Katie's family to a relative who was accused and then exonerated during the Salem witch trials. That wasn't it, Katie said. She was indifferent to gender, and in some ways she thought a boy would be preferable given that we already had all the clothes and gear. She just felt like our family could use one more child.

I still thought she was crazy, in part because Ben was our easiest child, and it seemed to me we should quit while we were ahead. To put off a real conversation about the topic, I made a point of waiting until the absolute height of chaos in our house—say, for example, a Saturday morning at seven o'clock when all three boys were up, two were melting down, and a third was nowhere to be found. And then I would say, "You know what would really round out this picture? A newborn!"

That bought me another year. Katie, however, remained undeterred. But we were clearly stuck, as Katie had made up her mind, and so had I. And then she pulled out the perfect question. "Couldn't we at least talk it through, and talk about what it would mean for our family?" So we talked it through, and then talked some more. And just two short years later, I finally came around. A bit more than nine months after that, Phebe came around as well. Katie was right. I couldn't imagine our family without Phebe. It was indeed incomplete without her.

Like the second essential question, "Couldn't we at least . . . ?" forms the core of a series of questions rather than one specific and complete question. Regardless of the variety of ways this question can be posed, at its core, asking "Couldn't we at least . . . ?" is a good way to get unstuck. It is a way to get past disagreement to form some consensus, as in, "Couldn't we at least agree?" It's also a way to get started even when you're not entirely sure where you will finish, as in: "Couldn't we at least begin?" No matter its specific form, asking questions that begin with "Couldn't we at least . . . ?" is the way to make progress.

To begin, asking "Couldn't we at least agree?" is a way to find common ground. The key to maintaining healthy and productive relationships is consensus—whether in politics, business, marriage, or friendship. Asking "Couldn't we at least agree?" especially in the midst of an argument, is a good way to pause, step back, and look for some areas of agreement. After taking a step back and finding some consensus, you might have just what you need to take two steps forward, which is just how progress often works: one step back, two steps forward.

Seeking common ground is especially important today. The explosion of information fueled by the internet and social media should in theory help bring us into contact and engagement with ideas, facts, and beliefs that challenge our own, which in turn should help us moderate our views and keep an open mind. In reality, the opposite is happening.

Studies of social media, Facebook in particular, show that we are creating virtual gated communities, where those with like-minded views only share information that confirms their beliefs. Traditional media, meanwhile, increasingly cater to segments of the population. Conservatives watch Fox News; liberals watch MSNBC. Both groups find confirmation for their existing opinions. Our virtual worlds are becoming so segmented that we can even choose from different broadcasts of the same sporting event—one that favors the home team or one that favors the visiting team. More and more, we can choose to see only what we want to see.

This is unfortunate, and dangerous, because of a phenomenon social scientists call "group polarization." When like-minded individuals get together, online or in real life, they tend to reinforce each other's views. They not only increase the strength of each other's convictions, but they often lead each other, intentionally or not, to take even more extreme positions. If you dislike the New York Yankees, for example, and you only hang around with others who are equally misguided, you are likely to become even more convinced that the Yankees are a bad and morally corrupt team. In fact, you are likely to take it a step further and begin to believe that the Yankees are an evil blight on the national pastime. I have seen this happen at Fenway Park in Boston, and, as a Yankees fan, I can tell you it's not pretty.

Asking "Couldn't we at least agree?" is a way to push back against polarization and extremism, because it is an invitation to find some areas of consensus. If you can find some common ground with others, especially those with different views, you are likely to see the world as a more nuanced place. At the very least, you are less likely to demonize those with whom you disagree. Take the Red Sox and Yankees again. Derek Jeter recently retired from the

Yankees; he was an outstanding player and an admirable person on and off the field. David Ortiz retired from the Red Sox at the end of the 2016 season. Big Papi, as he is called, was also a great player and rightly beloved. To find common ground among Yankees and Red Sox fans, bringing up Jeter and Big Papi is usually all you need, as fans on both sides of the divide usually admire Jeter and Big Papi. Once those two are part of the conversation, it lowers the temperature of any disagreement.

The question "Couldn't we at least agree?" works just as well with disputes about the Constitution as it does with baseball, as my friend and law school roommate Doug Kendall showed. For decades, liberals and conservatives disagreed about how to interpret the Constitution. Conservatives argued that judges should follow the original intent of the Constitution; whatever the framers thought the Constitution meant centuries ago is what it should mean today. Because this approach seemed to preclude the possibility that the Constitution could adapt over time, liberals rejected it, arguing for a "living Constitution" that could be updated by judges to fit modern times. Conservatives attacked the living Constitution approach as giving judges too much discretion, while liberals attacked the original intent approach as putting judges in a straitjacket sewn centuries ago.

Doug saw the obvious weaknesses in both approaches. He also saw an opening to advance his own view. He challenged the liberal view by asking, "Couldn't we at least agree that everyone should care about the actual meaning of the words in the Constitution?" And he challenged the conservative view by asking, "Couldn't we at least agree that a lot of important provisions in the Constitution are open-ended and establish general principles rather than concrete and specific rules? And couldn't we at least agree that the application of those general principles might change over time as circumstances, facts, and values change?" If you adopted a general principle that you will only eat healthy food, for example, you would be acting consistently with that principle if you changed what you ate over time as the science of nutrition revealed that some foods you thought were healthy were not, and vice versa. Doug argued that the Constitution worked the same way, and that you could indeed be faithful to its principles even if the application of those principles changed over time in light of new facts.

To advance this view of the Constitution, Doug created the Constitutional Accountability Center (CAC), a public interest group based in Washington, DC. CAC participated in cases, produced reports about the original meaning of key provisions in the Constitution, and became involved in judicial appointments. In a relatively short period of time, Doug and his colleagues established CAC as one of the leading voices in debates about the Constitution, and in the process helped change the conversation about the Constitution. Liberal lawyers and judges are showing much more interest in the original meaning of the Constitution, and they are now joined in healthy debates with their conservative colleagues about that meaning. More generally, there is a deeper appreciation that the Constitution—as amended over two centuries—is itself a document that has evolved to establish and enshrine principles of equality alongside principles of liberty. And along the way, Doug earned the respect and admiration of liberal and conservative lawyers alike.

To be sure, Doug's move was in part strategic. He believed that if liberals would actually take on conservatives over the true meaning of the language in the Constitution, they would often prevail. In this sense, asking "Couldn't we at least agree?" was both a call to find some common ground and the first step in an effort to win a larger battle over the meaning of the Constitution. In a way, Doug's approach was similar to Katie's approach when she asked me if we could at least talk about what it would mean to have a fourth child. Both Doug and Katie believed that finding some common ground was a first step toward persuading others to their views. And both were remarkably effective in doing just that.

Asking "Couldn't we at least agree?" will not resolve all disagreements, of course, but it can at least reduce their scope. Finding some common ground, in other words, can help isolate true areas of disagreement. This is especially helpful in preventing opposing sides on a particular issue from wasting time questioning the motives of their opponents, which happens far too frequently in public debates. Education debates, sadly, are a prime example.

You might think that those working in education would start from the premise that everyone in the field cares about the welfare of kids. Instead, warring sides in education debates are constantly questioning each other's motives. Those who favor charter schools, for example, are routinely accused of wanting to privatize public education and turn it over to hedge fund billionaires. Those who support teachers' unions are similarly maligned as supposedly caring more about the welfare of teachers than the children they teach.

This all-too-common approach to education debates is both poisonous and unproductive. To assert that those who disagree with you must have dubious or immoral goals is basically to announce that there's nothing left to discuss. If it were instead possible to begin with an honest conversation about values and goals, and to discover some agreement about those values and goals, education debates might actually be edifying. Again, I am not at all suggesting that simply asking "Couldn't we at least agree that we all care about the welfare of kids?" will resolve every difference among education warriors. But it might remove some acrimony and lead to constructive, rather than destructive, disagreements and debates.

In addition to inviting some agreement, asking "Couldn't we at least . . . ?" is also a great way to get moving, even when you don't have a fully formed plan. As the astute philosopher Mary Poppins recognized, "A job begun is a job half done." (Easy for her to say, given that she could magically move objects without touching them, but still, it's good advice.) Too often—whether because of procrastination, fear, or a desire for perfection—we hesitate to begin a project at home or at work if we cannot see precisely how or when it will end.

Yet sometimes the most important decision you can make is the decision to get started. One of my favorite quotes, sometimes attributed to the German writer Goethe, is this: "Whatever you can do or dream you can, begin it. Boldness has genius, power, and magic in it." I have seen the wisdom of this observation in both my personal and professional life.

Katie and I had always wanted to live abroad for a year with our kids. We thought it would be a great experience for them, and we believed it would bring us closer as a family. Life crept up on us, however, and several years ago, we realized we needed to do it soon or not do it all. When Katie and I also realized that we couldn't go away for an entire year, we considered giving up on the idea altogether. But eventually we decided that we could go away for "at least" a semester during my sabbatical, and we ultimately picked New Zealand. As soon as we fully committed to going, all sorts of things fell into place. I got an appointment as a visiting professor at the University of Auckland. We found a great public school for our kids, a place to live, and a car to drive. Though shorter than we had originally planned, our stay in New Zealand was one of the most enriching and rewarding five months in our life as a family. All because we asked "Couldn't we at least . . . ?" instead of giving up on the idea altogether.

Asking this question has also been a useful way to help my kids overcome fear when trying new things. Skiing is one example. I love to ski, and I selflessly decided to teach my kids to ski in the hope that they would get hooked, and then I would have the perfect excuse to go on ski trips. But skiing is a little overwhelming at first. The combination of strange gear, the size of the mountains, and the cold weather can cause new skiers—of any age, really—to be less than enthusiastic or adventurous. I discovered if I asked "Couldn't we at least . . . ?" when trying to nudge them to try something new, it often worked. So when they were afraid of the chair lift, I would say, "Couldn't we at least go over to see what it looks like?" Or when they were afraid of going down certain trails, I would say, "Couldn't we at least ski to the top of the trail and take a look down?"

This didn't always work, to be sure. "Couldn't we at least . . . ?" is an essential question, not a miracle question. But it was often just the question my kids needed to hear in order to help them take the next step. Sometimes, just seeing the object of your fear up close, rather than simply in your imagination, can help you overcome it. Asking "Couldn't we at least take a look?" can nudge you and others to do just that.

On the professional front, as dean I have never once regretted asking "Couldn't we at least get started?" on something—whether it was a new project or new initiative. I have discovered, consistent with Goethe's observation, that once you commit to something, you often end up mobilizing a stream of resources, ideas, and assistance that you never imagined would come your way.

Perhaps the best example of this came two years ago when my colleagues and I at the Education School decided to start a campus-wide conversation on the theme of "fulfilling the promise of diversity." We started this conversation for two primary reasons.

First, we did not have any common courses among our thirteen master's programs, which I thought was unfortunate for a professional school. Students in separate programs would never be brought together to focus on a particular body of knowledge, a common set of questions, or a cluster of specific skills. But, as a new dean, this was not something I could change right away. It did seem, though, that we could *at least* have a campus-wide conversation about a common topic, featuring lectures, panels, student-led projects, and faculty workshops, all focused on the topic of diversity.

Second, we chose diversity as a topic because the world of education—like the world in general— is becoming more diverse, and we thought it was important to prepare all of our students to work productively and to be successful leaders in the field. Diversity has the potential to make institutions and organizations stronger, but it also has the potential to create divisions. This conversation was aimed at understanding how to ensure that diversity is a source of strength rather than a source of division. It would also help all of us become more comfortable having hard conversations about race, identity, and equity—conversations that we insist are necessary but too often put off to the future.

I was also motivated to have a conversation on this particular topic because of an experience I had as a law student at the University of Virginia. A good friend, Ted Small, who is also a hero of mine, noticed that black and white law students at UVA self-segregated and largely kept to themselves. As a black student at Harvard, he had dealt with similar issues as an undergraduate, but the situation at UVA seemed even more severe. He suggested that we create a biracial group of ten law students who would meet monthly, over dinner, to discuss topics related to race.

We called the group "Students United to Promote Racial Awareness," or "SUPRA" for short. *Supra* is a Latin legal term, so the acronym doubled as a law-nerd joke. When Ted started the group, he had no real idea where the conversation would lead, but he thought—and I agreed—that it was important to do something. In a very real sense, he was asking "couldn't we at least" get ten students together to talk about these issues and maybe show that black and white law students can discuss hard issues together and perhaps become real friends in the process? By the time we graduated, our group had shared a lot of meals and a lot of conversations— some difficult, some challenging, others humorous and lighthearted. We emerged as friends, and our example helped spur a dozen additional SUPRA groups to form among our fellow law students. Although I did not fully appreciate it at the time, participating in SUPRA was one of the most formative and significant experiences I have ever had. To this day, I continue to rely on it as a guide, including in our community conversation at Harvard.

Our conversation at the Education School produced mixed results. On the plus side, it quickly became clear that there was a great deal of interest in this topic among students, faculty, and staff. On the other hand, it also became clear over the course of the year that we were not sufficiently organized to meet the demands of this topic. Some students rightly complained that they weren't sure where the conversation was headed and that there was not enough structure to it. They also believed, again rightly so, that we were not doing enough.

So we continued the conversation the next year. We provided more structure to the conversation; brought in more speakers; assigned a common reading; and added more than a dozen courses on race, diversity, and equity to our curriculum. This conversation also carried over into a redoubled effort to diversify our faculty and staff. It led to renewed attention and effort on the part of faculty to create inclusive and rigorous classroom experiences. And it enabled us to tap into the talent and expertise among our doctoral students, who led seminars and discussion groups, as well as workshops for faculty.

At the end of two years, what started as a loosely organized conversation had become an important part of the school's identity, across a range of contexts—from the classrooms to faculty hiring to the work environment for staff. The conversation is not over, and there is still plenty of work to do. But by committing to starting this conversation, we set in motion forces that have, I believe, made our school stronger and helped us better prepare our students to be leaders of diverse and equitable schools and organizations.

By highlighting this example, I do not mean to suggest that everything we have pursued at the Education School has been successful. Hardly. But even efforts that failed or were disappointing had something to teach us. Getting started does not guarantee success, but it does guarantee that you will not live with regret about failing to try, which is the last point of this chapter.

When you ask "Couldn't we at least . . . ?" you are essentially suggesting that you and others try to do something, whether it is to come to some agreement or to get started on something. If you don't ask this question, you are less likely to try. And failing to try, I believe, is the source of some of our deepest regrets—indeed, this is why I talked about the sin of omission in my second graduation speech at Harvard. I believe that what we don't do often haunts us more than what we actually do.

I am certainly not the first or only one to recognize this. Bonnie Ware, a nurse who cared for dying patients, published a book about the most common regrets her patients expressed. The number one regret was failing to pursue their dreams—failing, essentially, to try or to get started.

My own experience with this particular source of regret is not linked to pursuing a dream, but instead connected to my mother's death. My mother fell and broke her hip in August of 2009. At seventy-one, she was relatively young but had already endured a number of maladies that made her somewhat frail and vulnerable. Over a torturous five-week period after her fall, she suffered from one complication after another. There were a few times when I thought she was not receiving the care she needed. But, for a number of reasons, I didn't push the doctors to do more, and I didn't look for ways to get her to a different hospital or a different team of doctors. Five weeks after she fell, she suffered a series of strokes and died in the hospital while my sister and I held her hand.

Everyone around me assured me that the doctors had done all they could and that I had as well. But I didn't feel that way. I didn't blame the doctors, but I blamed myself for not pushing harder or doing more. Essentially, I blamed myself for never asking, "Couldn't we at least get a second opinion?"

Maybe the result would have been the same, but it's impossible to know, which is a heavy weight to bear. That's the problem with not trying—you will never know what the outcome might have been. Even if you think the result would have been the same, that's only a small comfort. When it comes to helping your friends and family, what you want most is to believe that you tried everything you could to help.

That is a sad story, I realize, but it has made me even more certain that the attempt is often more important than the result. I am confident, from my own experience, that every time you attempt to lend a hand, or to right a wrong, or to speak up, you will feel better—about the world and about yourself. When you act, you may make a mistake; when you speak, you may say the wrong thing. But it is much better to fail while daring greatly than to be a bystander, to borrow a line from Teddy Roosevelt. If you fail, often the worst thing that can happen is that you will have a funny story to tell. I have never heard a single funny story about failing to try.

Because it helps break logjams, whether created by disagreement, fear, procrastination, or lethargy, and whether created by external obstacles or internal ones, the question "Couldn't we at least . . . ?" sparks movement. It is the question that also recognizes that journeys are often long and uncertain, that problems will not be solved with one conversation, and that even the best efforts will not always work. At the same time, however, it is the question that recognizes you have to begin somewhere. It is the question that nudges you and others to the starting line. It is the question, as I said at the opening, at the heart of all progress, and for that reason—as Phebe and our entire, complete family can attest—it is absolutely essential to ask.

CHAPTER FOUR

How Can I Help?

Luckily for all of us, many people are interested in helping others; some devote their careers and lives to it. Not everyone is so inclined, of course, and most people are self-interested at least some of the time. An evolutionary biologist or psychologist might say that we are *always* self-interested, and that our effort to help others is simply our attempt to feel good about ourselves. Regardless of our motivations, however, a remarkable number of us help out our colleagues, family, friends, and even strangers.

Although admirable, there is a risk in helping others, which is related to the possibility that helping can actually be selfish. That risk lies in falling prey to what some call "the savior complex." This is just what it sounds like—an attitude or stance toward the world where you believe you are the expert who can swoop in to save others. It is a lopsided approach to helping, in which the helper believes she has all of the answers, knows just what to do, and that the person or group in need has been waiting for a savior to come along.

While this is a genuine problem, we should not let the real pitfalls of the savior complex extinguish one of the most humane instincts there is—the instinct to lend a hand. The trick is to help others without believing yourself to be, or acting like you are, their savior.

All of which is to say that *how* you help matters just as much as that you *do* help, which is why it is essential to begin by asking, "How can I help?" If you start with this question, you are asking, with humility, for direction. You are recognizing that others are experts in their own lives, and you are affording them the opportunity to remain in charge, even if you are providing some help.

I recently heard a great story on *The Moth*, which underscored the importance of asking *how* you can help. *The Moth* is a radio program and podcast that features true stories, told live by people from around the world. The stories are riveting, including a recent one from a woman in her eighties, who explained how she valued her independence. She loved the fact that she had always taken care of herself and that she could still do so into her eighth decade. And then she had a stroke.

While she was in the hospital, her neighbors in her New York City apartment building made some minor renovations to her apartment to make it easier for her to live there with a walker, which she would need after her stroke. At first she was taken aback, as she was cordial but not good friends with her neighbors. But their gesture of goodwill inspired her to recognize that some dependence on others could actually enrich her life, especially if she reciprocated. So she hung a sign on her apartment door welcoming her neighbors to come in for a chat. She then recounted how her neighbors often came by to talk and emphasized with gratitude that, when they offered to help, they always asked *how* they could help. By asking her how they could help, she explained, they were allowing her to retain her independence and dignity.

In addition to showing respect, asking how you can help is also—not surprisingly—likely to make your assistance more effective. My wife, Katie, asks this question, and pays attention to the answer, as well as anyone I know. I could relay many examples, but I'll share just two.

In 1996, Katie and I took a bike trip from Nairobi, Kenya, to Victoria Falls, Zimbabwe. The trip, which covered over a thousand miles, took us six weeks to complete. It was a remarkable journey from start to finish. We traveled with a haphazardly organized tour group, and our fellow cyclists were mostly British. One, whom I will call Nelson, was in his sixties. Tall, lanky, quite pale, and with a slightly eccentric personality, Nelson looked and behaved like the longtime British librarian that he was. When we reached Victoria Falls, we all took hotel rooms to celebrate the completion of our adventure and made plans to meet for dinner. When we went to pick up Nelson, he came to his hotel door quite incoherent. He was, essentially, babbling.

Our group thought that Nelson had celebrated the end of a long journey with too much to drink, so we let him be and went to dinner. All during dinner, though, Katie continued to wonder about Nelson, insisting to me that something didn't seem right. So we went back to his hotel room after dinner, and when he came to the door, Katie asked him, "How can we help you, Nelson? You seem like you're having some trouble." In between calling out random letters and numbers, like he was playing bingo or shelving library books, Nelson regained a moment of clarity and said, "I feel a touch off. My head is throbbing."

Katie took him to the local hospital and helped him get in to see a doctor, which was no small feat. It turned out that Nelson had cerebral malaria, which is deadly if not treated. The doctor told Katie, in all seriousness, that she had gotten Nelson there just in time. Nelson was helicoptered to a larger hospital in Harare, where he received the treatment he needed. Had Katie not asked Nelson how we could help, and had she just assumed we already knew his problem, Nelson would likely have died in his hotel room.

A slightly less dramatic example comes from a case Katie and her colleagues worked on recently. A special education attorney, Katie works at a clinic at Harvard Law School. With her colleagues and law students, she represents poor children who are eligible for special education but are not receiving the services to which they are entitled under state and federal law. Too often in these situations, school officials, doctors, or attorneys will tell the kids and their families what they need. Katie and her colleagues make sure to understand what the kids and their families actually want by asking, in one way or another, "How can we help?"

One of her clients, whom I will call Robert, came to her when he was eighteen. Robert had not been to school in about two years. He had only a fraction of the credits he needed to graduate high school, yet he was very capable academically, with an IQ in the ninetieth percentile.

Robert struggled with significant (and undiagnosed) anxiety, which at times overwhelmed his ability to function. When he was younger, he was frequently absent from school and then stopped going altogether when his father was diagnosed with an advanced brain tumor. Because his mother was working full time, much of the burden of caring for his father fell on Robert.

The school officials considered Robert's case as one of willful truancy. They concluded that Robert simply didn't want to attend school anymore. Thinking they were helping him, school officials advised him to drop out and earn his GED. Because Robert could easily pass the test and then attend a community college, this seemed like an obvious solution.

But this was not what Robert wanted, which Katie and her colleagues learned by listening to him. Taking the GED would not help him build skills to manage his anxiety. Besides, Robert had loftier aspirations. He wanted to graduate high school with a regular diploma and go on to a four-year college. He understood that this would be a challenge, given that he would be much older than his classmates. But he was determined.

Katie and her colleagues took the case. Working with Robert, they ultimately convinced the relevant school officials that Robert's absence from school stemmed from an anxiety disorder that needed to be addressed. Robert ended up attending a small public high school for students with emotional disabilities, earned straight As his first year there, and is on his way to graduating. All because Katie and her colleagues asked "How can we help?" and then listened to—and respected—Robert's answer.

While Katie instinctively knows to ask this question, I had to be taught its importance. I learned my lesson from a client I will call Patrick, a Cameroonian journalist. I was practicing law in Newark, New Jersey, at a law firm with the memorable but unfortunate name of Crummy, Del Deo.

This firm sponsored a public interest fellowship and allowed the fellows, of which I was one, to work solely on pro bono cases. It was a great job, because it meant I could work on whatever cases interested me the most. Patrick's case intrigued me.

Patrick was seeking political asylum. While broadcasting on a state-owned television station about election results in Cameroon, Patrick made the brave and dangerous decision to report, live from the field, on rampant election fraud committed by the government. By the time he got back to his office, police were waiting for him. They took Patrick to prison and, for months, brutally tortured him. On several occasions, they came close to killing him. His mother eventually bribed a prison guard, who released Patrick in the middle of the night, under the cover of darkness. Patrick then began an odyssey across several continents that ended with his entering the United States under a false passport. When a customs official questioned Patrick about his passport, he admitted it was fake. Though he tried to explain he was seeking asylum, Patrick was arrested and sent to a detention center in Newark, which housed unauthorized immigrants caught at the U.S. border.

A human rights group identified Patrick's case and sent it my way. I knew that to satisfy the legal standard for obtaining asylum, the applicant needed to show he had a "credible fear of persecution." I set out to get the facts from Patrick that would allow me to make his case. This took a fairly long time, and the asylum process itself moved at a glacial pace. As the process continued to drag on, Patrick grew increasingly despondent. I thought we were making progress, albeit slowly, but Patrick saw endless day after endless day pass by.

During one interview, when Patrick offered very brief answers to my questions, I stopped and said that he seemed depressed. And I (finally) asked him if there was something I could do to help. He said, "I really need to get out of this place. It's killing me to have come all this way only to be in prison again." I knew that being detained was not his first choice, and was not anyone's first choice, but I thought it would be a small price to pay if he received asylum. But Patrick's statement jolted me. I started researching more about the asylum process and learned that those awaiting an asylum hearing could be released to a family willing to take them in. Katie and I could not host him, because we lived with our newborn son in a tiny apartment, which literally couldn't fit another body. But a generous colleague and her family volunteered to host Patrick, so I temporarily put aside Patrick's asylum case and worked to get him released.

Within a couple of weeks, Patrick's petition for release was granted, and he went to live with his host family. He stayed with them for several months while we continued to prepare for his hearing, which I finally came to realize should be Patrick's chance, not mine, to tell his story. So with the expert assistance of a colleague, we worked to help Patrick tell his story.

Patrick ultimately received asylum, and he went on to find a good job in New Jersey and create a new life. A few years later, Patrick asked me to serve as the best man at his wedding. The memory of his wedding still brings tears to my eyes. When I later asked him why he wanted me to be his best man, he said, "Because you were my first friend here. You listened to me."

Asking how you can help is also an effective way of nudging others to identify, express, and confront their own problems. This is sometimes understandably hard to do, as Atul Gawande describes movingly in *Being Mortal,* in which he recounts the difficult choices advanced cancer patients must make about their own care. Because facing your own mortality is indescribably difficult, and because doctors naturally want to save patients, it is hard for doctors and patients to have candid discussions about the end of life. But as Gawande points out, cancer patients and their families most need someone to help guide them with candor and compassion. It occurred to me when reading this book that if doctors asked the patients how they could help, before simply pointing out all of the various interventions they could perform, they would in a way force the question, which only the patient can answer: What do you want to do? How do you want to spend what may be your last months of life? How do you want to make that decision—what information would be useful, for example, and who else would you like to include in the conversation?

Asking how you can help is equally effective in less dire circumstances, though for similar reasons. If you ask others how you can help, you are inviting them to take some ownership of their own problems. For this reason, it is a useful question to ask friends, family, and colleagues. It is a particularly useful question, I have found, to ask kids and young adults.

In between college and law school, I spent a winter working at a children's ski school in Colorado. I had no training as an instructor, so I spent most of the winter as an inside aide, moving outside to be an instructor for beginning skiers only when most of the other instructors had left for the season. While working with the inside staff, I made lunches, helped kids get on and off their gear, wiped noses, found mittens, and tried to soothe frayed nerves of parents and kids alike. I also made a lot of hot chocolate. The kids were quite young, and some were overwhelmed by it all, just as my own kids were years later when I tried to teach them how to ski. At the ski school, we tried to help as much as we could, which often meant that we made suggestion after suggestion about what the kids could and should do to get comfortable.

Most of the time these suggestions worked, but sometimes they just made the kids more agitated. It was as if the obvious futility of our suggestions just confirmed for them how hopeless their situations were. I remember one particularly obstinate seven-year-old boy, who refused to go out after lunch for his afternoon ski lesson. I made suggestion after suggestion—tighten your boots, pull on your mittens, wear your goggles, put on your scarf. With each suggestion, he became more disagreeable, until completely exasperated, I finally asked, "Okay, this isn't working, so maybe you can tell me how I can help you?"

To my surprise, that question made him pause. He looked around, and then he very quietly said, "I'm still hungry." I made him another PB&J sandwich and sat with him while he ate. He was definitely hungry, but I also think he needed a mental health break. I didn't anticipate it at the time, but by asking him to tell me what he needed, I shifted the burden to him to identify and begin to address what, exactly, was bothering him.

I have found this question very effective as a parent and when working with struggling or unhappy students. As parents (and teachers), you try to help solve problems, both big and small. Very often, you think you know what the solution is, so you offer your idea—or a whole slew of ideas. Yet sometimes offering solutions simply fuels the anxiety or stubbornness that your kids or students are feeling, just as occurred with the boy in ski school. If you instead listen patiently and silently to their concerns and complaints, and then ask how you can help, it changes the conversation. It usually causes my own kids to pause. They think about whether I can actually help them and, if so, how. More often than not, they eventually tell me that I can't really do anything. But in saying this they are already starting to figure out the problem for themselves. What they most needed to do was vent, get some sympathy, and figure out a solution for themselves.

The need to vent is not confined to kids. My cousin Tracy, who is as funny as she is wise, told me a story once of coming home after a really frustrating day at work and recounting her day to her boyfriend. Instead of listening to the entire story, her boyfriend immediately started offering ideas about what she could have done to solve her problems. She found this maddening. "I didn't want him to solve my problems," she told me. "I just wanted him to listen and understand that I had a crappy day at work."

If you ask friends, family members, or colleagues how you can help, you are not offering to solve their problems with specific suggestions. Instead, you are validating that they have a real problem and letting them know you are available to help, if need be. You are showing both sympathy and empathy, which is sometimes all someone needs. Put differently, in asking how you can help, sometimes you already have.

Finally, if you ask *how* you can help, you are entering a conversation and a relationship on more equal footing. You are likely to be open, as you should be, to the possibility that the person you are offering to help will likely have something to offer you in return. After all, you are inviting them to teach you enough about their situation or their lives to enable you to help them. In this way, asking how you can help is an invitation to begin a genuine relationship, one based on the notion of reciprocity.

I came to appreciate this point when I worked as a volunteer for a few months in rural Kentucky, right after I finished at the ski school in Colorado and just before I started law school. I worked with a Catholic volunteer organization, and I thought I would be going door-to-door in Appalachia, offering whatever assistance I could. I can't completely remember what compelled me to volunteer, but I'm sure a touch of the savior complex motivated me. It's embarrassing to recollect, but I expect I believed that at age nineteen, with no relevant experience, I could somehow help the rural poor of Appalachia.

To my surprise, I was not sent door to door but was instead assigned to a small group home for kids with disabilities. Most of them were very young and had life-limiting ailments. None were likely to live into their teens. One of the residents, however, was a vibrant teenage girl with Down syndrome, whom I will call Cindy.

As soon as I stepped into the home, which was a neat, bright, and cozy one-story ranch house, Cindy came and grabbed my hand. "You're pretty," she told me. After I made some lame attempt to say something funny in response, she said, "Jim, you're so funny." From that point on, every morning when I arrived, Cindy would grab my hand and say some version of "Jim, you're pretty. And you're so funny."

I spent most of the day dealing with the basic necessities of bathing, dressing, feeding, and entertaining the kids. The small staff who worked there graciously welcomed my help and patiently taught me what I needed to know. Most of it was fairly straightforward, but there was one boy who had a feeding tube, which needed to be cleaned regularly. A colleague showed me how to do it, but I was still nervous the first time I tried to clean it, worrying that I might hurt the boy. Cindy saw me struggling, came over, and took charge. I looked at my colleague with an expression that asked if this was okay, and she smiled and nodded. Cindy expertly cleaned the feeding tube while telling me it was easy.

From that point on, I noticed that Cindy knew, as much as anyone else, how to help the other kids. She knew the food they liked, how they liked to be lifted from their wheelchairs for a bath or change of clothes, how to comb their hair, what songs they liked to hear. She became my teacher and guide. Because the kids couldn't speak, I couldn't ask them how I could help them. But I could ask Cindy, or simply follow her lead.

One girl at the home captured my heart. I'll call her Susie. Not quite two years old, Susie had beautiful blue eyes, dimples, wispy blonde hair, and an easy smile. She had spinal cord damage and could not sit up. She was also deaf and very quiet. But when you looked at her she would hold your gaze like she was intently studying your face. I wasn't quite sure what I could do to entertain or comfort her. One morning, Cindy saw me standing over Susie's crib. Cindy walked over, took my hand and guided it to Susie's hand. Susie took my hand and used it to caress her cheek, smiling the whole time. "She likes that," Cindy said, herself smiling.

To say I learned more than I helped would be a gross understatement. This was not why I went, but this was the result. I learned in Kentucky not to underestimate those with "disabilities," like Cindy, who taught me more about the kids I was trying to help than I would have ever learned on my own, and who became not only my teacher but my friend. I learned from the children and staff that small joys can exist alongside real tragedy. The stories of the kids who lived in the home were heartbreaking, but it was not a sad place. It was a place filled with love and caring.

Perhaps most of all, I learned about acceptance and humility. I could entertain the kids, help feed them, and care for them. But I could not do much more. I certainly couldn't change the trajectory of their lives, nor could anyone there. So I followed the lead of Cindy and concentrated on that day, that moment, and that child. I tried to provide some comfort and, where I could, some joy.

It was at once a hard lesson to learn and a liberating one, and it has stayed with me. So much so that when Katie and I were married, I asked my friend Roger to read Robert Frost's "A Prayer in Spring" at the ceremony. Roger had been with me in Kentucky, and it was there that I first came across this poem, which captures well what Cindy and the other kids had taught me.

The poem begins:

Oh, give us pleasure in the flowers today;
And give us not to think so far away
As the uncertain harvest; keep us here
All simply in the springing of the year

After encouraging the reader to enjoy the orchards, bees, and birds surrounding her, the poem ends:

For this is love and nothing else is love,
The which it is reserved for God above
To sanctify to what far ends he will,
But which it only needs that we fulfill.

In other words, who knows what all of this ultimately means, but our most important task for now is to notice and appreciate the fleeting beauty around us. In my experience, if you offer to help others and leave yourself open to their help in return, you will come to appreciate that, in Frost's words, "this is love, and nothing else is love."

It is for all of these reasons that "How can I help?" is an essential question. It is the question that forms the base of all good relationships. It is a question that signals that you care. It signals a willingness to help. But it also signals respect, humility, and the likelihood that, in the end, it is you who will be helped just as much.

CHAPTER FIVE

What Truly Matters?

The fifth and final essential question asks, "What truly matters?" This is the question that can just as effectively guide you through a meeting with colleagues as it can guide you through the biggest decisions in your life. It forces you to get to the heart of issues at work or school, and to the heart of your own convictions, beliefs, and goals in life. It's the question that can help you separate the truly important from the trivial and can help you maneuver through the minutiae in pursuit of the momentous.

In retrospect, this is the question a lot of us should have asked on the morning that our second son, Sam, was born. This is a cautionary tale—though it thankfully has a happy ending. And I promise it is the last childbirth tale in the book.

While pregnant with Sam, Katie heard time and again that the second child can come quickly—meaning that the labor can be very short. This came as welcome news to Katie, given the long ordeal she went through when delivering our first son, Will. When Katie awoke with labor pains at four o'clock in the morning on November 29, 1998, I knew we needed to get moving right away. Katie's college friend, an OB-GYN, happened to be staying over that night, and she urged us to drive immediately to the hospital. Incurably responsible, Katie wanted to make sure our dogs, cat, and two horses were fed before we left. She also decided to take a shower.

When we finally got into the car, Katie's contractions were already coming fairly quickly and painfully. I sped to the hospital, nearly hitting a deer along the way. By the time we arrived, Katie was in active labor. For reasons I can't quite explain, other than to say I wasn't thinking clearly, I drove past the entrance to the emergency room and into the outdoor parking garage for hospital visitors. Because it was so early, the parking gate was up and no attendant was around. I thought, *If we go in this entrance, they won't know when we entered and we will likely have to pay an arm and a leg for parking.* I know, I know: dumb move.

I backed out of the garage and went to another entrance, also with the gate up. But this time I decided to take my chances, in part because Katie was now saying, with a fair bit of certainty, that she was "GOING TO HAVE THIS BABY RIGHT NOW!" I tried to explain why this would not, actually, be a good idea. When I parked and went to help her, Katie repeated her intent to deliver Sam immediately and then added that she was pretty sure she could no longer walk. I thought of opening the hatch of our Subaru station wagon, having her lie down like cargo in the back, and then driving slowly with the hatch up to the emergency room, which was only about five hundred yards away yet seemed so far at the same time.

I ultimately half-carried, half-supported Katie down the stairs, having helpfully parked on the second level of the garage. When we got to the bottom of the stairs, Katie decided she just needed to lie down for a minute—on the sidewalk across the street from the emergency room. I calmly started screaming my head off, and luckily someone in the hospital heard us and brought us inside, Katie riding uncomfortably in a wheelchair.

At this point, Katie was doing all she could to prevent Sam from popping out, but for whatever reason she didn't find it helpful when I said, "Well, at least he's not stuck." As we entered the emergency room, an administrator greeted us and informed us that we needed to go to "triage," where they check to make sure it's not a false alarm before sending you to the delivery room. We promised, pretty emphatically, that Katie was not in false labor and that her screams of pain were genuine. But the administrator kept repeating that "Everyone goes to triage," in a pleasant but slightly menacing tone, which reminded me of Nurse Ratched in *One Flew Over the Cuckoo's Nest*. Because things usually didn't turn out so well when you crossed Nurse Ratched, I suggested we just go to triage. Quickly.

There we met the hapless medical resident on call, who greeted us without the sense of urgency that the situation seemed to warrant. After trying to exchange some pleasantries in between Katie's shouts of pain, he examined Katie and said with surprise, "Wow, I can almost see the baby's head! That's incredible!" And then after a slight pause to see if we appreciated how amazing it was that Katie was truly about to give birth, he added, "I think maybe we should get you to the delivery room."

A few minutes later, we were in the delivery room with the resident and a nurse, who was clearly more experienced than the resident. Katie was just as ready to have the baby as she had been ten minutes earlier, meaning that she was *really* ready. The medical resident, on the other hand, was clearly *not* ready. He looked to the nurse and began to list everything he might need for the delivery. "I'll need my safety glasses," he said, as the nurse looked skeptically back at him. "I'll need my booties," meaning those blue or green cloth covers that go over shoes, and "I'll need some water. To drink." At this point, the nurse looked over at me with a raised eyebrow, which prompted me to suggest, gently, "Doctor, I think maybe we need to focus here a bit. Katie is about to burst."

The nurse, thankfully, picked up on this theme and suggested, respectfully, that the attending physician was right next door. "I suggest we call the attending for a consult," the resident then said. The attending physician came right away. He walked directly over to Katie, spent about two minutes examining her, and said, "Alright, are you ready to have this baby?" Katie replied with some saltier version of, "Yes, that would be lovely." About five minutes later, Sam entered the world.

Looking back, it is fairly easy to identify a number of missteps by everyone involved, at least some of which could have been avoided by asking, "What truly matters?" The only thing that mattered for Katie and Sam was a healthy delivery. Yet everyone involved wasted precious time on distractions. Feeding the horses and taking a shower are good things to do on a daily basis, but not when you are about to have a baby. Not paying too much for parking? This is a perfectly admirable goal generally—and was a guiding principle in my father's life—but probably not so important when your wife is in labor. Sticking to bureaucratic procedures also didn't matter as much as ensuring the healthy delivery of a baby. Similarly, making sure you have your booties on before you deliver a baby might be a good idea in the abstract, but probably not worth it when time is of the essence.

As our misadventure with Sam illustrates, it is all too easy to lose sight of what truly matters. We may be too caught in routines to pay attention. We may lack confidence in our abilities and focus on largely irrelevant details rather than confront the difficult and challenging work in front of us. We may become so stressed that we become easily distracted or have trouble focusing. In each of these situations, it is useful to ask yourself what truly matters. Doing so can help you dispense with routines, muster the courage to face difficult work, and help you regain enough calm to identify what is truly important. Luckily, it all ended well with Sam, and it eventually became a funny story, though admittedly it took Katie (and her parents) a little while to appreciate the humor in our follies—okay, my follies. We had a number of conversations shortly after Sam was born where I said things like, "You have to admit that it was at least a little funny when I looked for cheap parking. Right? Right?"

Asking yourself and others what truly matters is equally useful in the workplace or at school. It enables you to cut through distractions, tangents, and irrelevant details and to stay focused on the real and important tasks that have to be completed. Think of the nurse who suggested calling the attending physician, or the attending physician himself, who within minutes knew exactly what the situation required. Both the nurse and doctor had clearly asked themselves a version of "What truly matters?" as they sized up the situation before them.

Or consider the example of my former boss, Chief Justice Rehnquist, who always kept his eye on the ball. As I mentioned in the first chapter, I spent a year as a law clerk for Chief Justice Rehnquist shortly after I graduated from law school. Part of my job, along with my two co-clerks, was to help prepare the chief justice (or "the Chief" as we called him) for oral arguments. To do so, we read the numerous briefs prepared by the lawyers for the parties to the case, as well as any additional briefs prepared for *amicus curiae*, or "friends of the court," which were usually advocacy groups who could offer some additional expertise or perspective on the issues involved. In total, each case involved hundreds of pages of written material, which the clerks and justices pored through in preparation for an hour-long oral argument.

Most other justices asked their clerks to prepare what were called "bench memos," which summarized the facts and procedural history of the case, as well as the arguments made in the various briefs. The memos usually concluded with an analysis of the merits of the case in addition to some areas for suggested questioning. We called them "bench memos" because the justices brought the memos to the "bench," where they sat during oral arguments. As you might imagine, the memos were quite long and took a great deal of time and effort to put together.

The Chief did not require us to write bench memos, which was one of the many unique and wonderful aspects of clerking for him. Instead, he prepared for oral arguments by taking a walk around the block with the clerk responsible for the case. The only slightly nerve-wracking aspect of this approach was the uncertain timing. (In my case, there was also the very real possibility that I might look like a total fool in front of the Chief Justice of the United States.) We knew we had to be ready by a particular date to have a conversation with the Chief about the case, but we didn't know exactly when, after that date, the phone would ring with an invitation to take a walk with him.

We walked around the block occupied by the Supreme Court, which is a large, ornate building just behind the Capitol Dome. The walks confirmed how anonymous most Supreme Court justices were, including the Chief. Only once did someone recognize him, and that was Linda Greenhouse, a *New York Times* reporter who covered the Supreme Court. On every walk, we would pass tourists who were visiting the Supreme Court, and they never recognized the Chief. I recall once, when we had to make our way through a crowd of rambunctious middle schoolers, that the Chief suggested to their teacher that she might want to keep her students from blocking the sidewalk. She responded with a look that suggested, pretty clearly, that you might want to mind your own business, old man. I smiled and thought, *If only she knew!*

During those walks, which usually lasted about twenty minutes, we would discuss the case and the upcoming oral argument. The Chief began by asking our view of the merits of the case, and then he would start asking questions. The questions went directly to the heart of the case. We spent no time on procedural details that had no bearing on the outcome, or on any other aspect of the case that would not influence the result. It was all wheat and no chaff; all substance and no fluff. The Chief and I did not always agree on the answers to the questions, as we saw the world quite differently. Indeed, I recall him asking me, in so many words, "Wait, what? You honestly believe that? I mean, you're not joking?" But there was no doubt that his questions were exactly the right ones to ask; they were akin to the kind of questions Justice Stevens asked at oral argument.

Admittedly, the Chief was truly exceptional in his ability to cut quickly through reams of information to identify key questions and issues. It is one of the reasons he was such a successful lawyer and selected to be a Supreme Court justice. He was also experienced, unlike the overwhelmed medical resident we met when Sam was born. By the time I clerked for him, the Chief had been on the Court for a couple of decades, so he had plenty of chances to hone his skill. Talent and experience undoubtedly helped him quickly identify what mattered most in the cases he heard.

Yet his mindset mattered as well. The Chief approached his whole life the same way he approached cases. He clearly thought about what truly mattered in every facet of his life. The Chief did not like to waste time. Years after clerking for the Chief, I came across a passage in a book by Tim Geithner, who served as treasury secretary under President Obama. The passage reminded me of the Chief. Not surprisingly, Secretary Geithner had to attend a lot of meetings, some of which were real and meant to make progress, and some of which were just for show. He got into the habit of walking into meetings called by others and asking, "Is this a real meeting or a fake meeting?" Geithner later chastised himself for being too impatient, but I find his question both hilarious and dead-on right. What clearly mattered to Geithner was getting work done, not doing things for show. The Chief felt the same way.

The Chief hated wasting time, I believe, because he had an almost endless array of hobbies and interests—including geography, history, Gilbert and Sullivan operas, swimming, meteorology, college football, tennis, painting, and writing. Even though he had one of the most demanding and important jobs in the world, which he took very seriously, he made time for these hobbies and remained deeply devoted to his family. He always managed to view the responsibilities of his office as one aspect of his life—a critical one, to be sure, but only one. Because there was so much he wanted to do, he knew he couldn't afford to waste any time.

I thought about the Chief's approach to life during a talk I attended by Randy Pausch at the University of Virginia in 2008. As you may recall,

Professor Pausch was a computer scientist at Carnegie Mellon who learned that he had pancreatic cancer, a terminal condition, in 2007. Shortly after he was diagnosed, he gave a lecture at Carnegie Mellon titled "The Last Lecture: Really Achieving Your Childhood Dreams." He then wrote a bestselling book expanding on the lecture. His talk at UVA was about the book.

I went expecting that I would hear a deeply philosophical lecture about the meaning of life from someone directly confronting his own mortality. Instead, to my surprise, the lecture was extremely practical, detailing ways to save time at work. Professor Pausch's underlying premise was that you should be as efficient as possible at work so that you can do all of the things outside of work that matter just as much, like spending time with family and friends, or pursuing hobbies and other passions. He was agnostic about what those things might be and wasn't interested in telling the audience what they should value. Instead, he was suggesting a sort of hypervigilant approach toward the question of what truly matters, where you constantly ask yourself this question in order to figure out practical strategies to help you live your life consistent with the answers to that question. Although I was initially disappointed by his lecture, I have come to realize the value in his advice, which made me even more appreciative of the example set by the Chief.

You do not need to be the chief justice of the United States to ask what truly matters or to benefit from its answer. My father, for example, never served as chief justice, but he figured out what truly mattered to him: his family. Nearly everything he did in his life came back to this touchstone principle. He worked at his job to provide for his family, not because he especially enjoyed it. (I still remember him shaking his head at my naïveté when I said I hoped to get a job I really loved, and him saying, "There's a reason it's called work.") When he was not working, my dad spent his time working around our house, attending my sister's and my various events, and trying to teach me home improvement skills that I still lack—like how to install a new electrical outlet, a lesson he abandoned after I kept shocking myself.

My dad also spent a lot of time hitting baseballs to me in our backyard. Throughout the spring and summer, we would spend hours together, him hitting ball after ball for me to field and occasionally giving me advice, which one time included, "Okay, just give the tooth to me and head back out there," after I had misjudged a line drive. "It was just a baby tooth," I remember him later telling my (slightly horrified) mom.

As he got older, my father grew sentimental, and he would get quietly emotional at momentous occasions like graduations and weddings. When I graduated from college, he said, with tears in his eyes, that he guessed I must have learned a thing or two fielding baseballs in the backyard. He meant it half-jokingly, but it was also his poignant way of acknowledging that he hadn't gone to college himself and of expressing his hope that he had nonetheless helped me along the way.

The baseball line became a running joke between us, which he repeated when I graduated from law school and whenever I started a new job or reached some sort of milestone. In 1997, a year before my dad died, I received an offer to teach law at the University of Virginia. Katie and I were new parents at the time. When I called my parents to tell them about the offer from UVA, my father predictably said I must have learned a lot by playing baseball with him in the backyard. I thought about our son

Will. Instead of just laughing off my father's remark, as I usually did, I told him, not knowing it would be my last chance, "I actually did learn a lot, Pop. I learned what it means to be a good father." I tried to say more, but he choked up and handed the phone to my mom.

In deciding that his family truly mattered to him, my father was not unique. I think most people who ask themselves what truly matters, in the grand scheme of their lives, would include family in their answer, regardless of how they define family. In fact, this last of the five essential questions is a bit different from the others in that the answers are fairly predictable, at least on the surface. My guess is that just about anyone who asks this question would identify family, friends, work, and perhaps kindness as things that truly matter to them.

I say this with some confidence because I have read a lot of memorials written to celebrate the life of someone who recently passed away. Law journals, which I read regularly as a law professor, often carry tributes to honor the work and life of a recently deceased colleague. Newspapers also carry long-form obituaries of notable people who have passed away. And after the terrorist attacks on the World Trade

Center, the *New York Times* devoted pages and pages of stories about men and women killed on 9/11, all of which I read. I have been fascinated by these tributes for a long time. In fact, I find these stories so compelling that, for years, I have suggested to anyone who will listen that there ought to be a funeral channel on cable television. But I digress.

What I have discovered in reading memorials is that every one of them usually hits on the four areas of life mentioned above: family, friends, work, and acts of kindness. You have to take these memorials with a grain of salt, obviously, because objective criticism is not a feature of this genre. In addition, if you read closely, you can tell when the writer is struggling to come up with an example for one of these four categories. But the writers almost always try, which signals to me the universal importance of these four core categories. The fact that memorial writers try to discuss these topics suggests that they believe these are the topics that truly matter—after all, you wouldn't spend a lot of time talking about aspects of the deceased's life that you thought were unimportant.

This doesn't mean that it's pointless to ask what truly matters because we already know the answers.

You may have additional categories. More importantly, within these broad categories, you still have to figure out for yourself what truly matters. In other words, you alone need to decide what truly matters about your work, your family, your friendships, and how to be kind. And you need to decide how to balance those values when they are in tension or in full-blown conflict, like the ever-present need to balance work and family.

Asking yourself "What truly matters?" before your memorial is written is a good way to take stock of your life, and for that reason it's a good question to ask each New Year. If, like me, you are lousy at keeping your annual resolutions, substituting a question for a resolution might not be a bad strategy. The key is to get beyond simply identifying the categories or topics that matter to you and to think through what is going well, what could go better, and why. I try to think, for example, how I could be a better husband, a better father, a better friend, and a better colleague. When my parents were still alive, I tried to think about how to be a better son. I still fall short, which is one of the reasons I continue to ask the question.

I'll close with one example involving my mother, which helps illustrate why identifying family as important is a good place to start, but it does not fully answer the question of what truly matters. I knew that my mother was important to me, but it took me a long time to realize that what truly mattered to her—and therefore to our relationship—was my forgiveness.

Through the bulk of my childhood and all of my adulthood, my mother was a recovered alcoholic. I appreciate the common notion of "once an alcoholic, always an alcoholic." But I describe my mother as a recovered alcoholic because after she stopped drinking, she never went back to it for the rest of her life. It took her going away, however, to stop.

When I was seven, my father convinced my mother to go into a residential rehabilitation facility, which she later referred to, not-so-lovingly, as "the drunk farm." My father could not afford to pay the fees, so he borrowed money from my mother's uncle, who had been fairly successful. She was gone for about six months, and while she was away, my father took care of my sister and me. This was back in the early 1970s, before many fathers were actively involved in the day-to-day details of parenting, and during a time when my family could not afford a regular babysitter. So it was a little touch and go.

I only have a few snapshots of memories from the time my mother was away. I remember my sister and I waking up at five thirty in the morning, so that we could be dropped off at a neighbor's house before school and my father could make it to work by six thirty. I remember that this neighbor, who had five kids of her own, used powdered milk for cereal and wouldn't let us watch television before school, neither of which thrilled me. I remember my mother writing me many letters, often in creative ways on the back of pictures she had painted, or in a spiral on a circular piece of paper. I remember really missing her at one of my little league baseball games. I remember watching a neighbor, who dropped me off at summer camp, pointing to me and clearly explaining to the counselor what was up with me and my mother. I remember crying then for the first and only time my mother was away. I remember having to go to my grandfather's house one Saturday when my dad went to visit my mom, protesting because it was the first day of the new fall season of cartoons, and my grandfather didn't have a television. And I remember the day my mother came home, and we threw her a party.

From that day forward, although it took me years to realize it, my mother was in some ways trying to make up for lost time. Like my father, my mother was remarkably dedicated to my sister and me. Our house was a fairly traditional one. My mother was a stay-at-home mom until my sister went to college, when she went back to work to help pay the tuition bills.

My mother was caring, smart, and talented. She baked every kind of pie and cake. Her desserts became legendary in our family and among our friends. She sewed and made us Halloween costumes every year; she knit sweaters, scarves, mittens, and hats; she crocheted; she did needlepoint. She also read two or three mystery novels each week and could finish the *New York Times* Sunday crossword puzzle in an hour. She drove us to every practice and game, and never missed one of the latter. She became the second mother to my friends and knew as much about their lives as I did. When my sister and I went away to college, and beyond, she unfailingly sent care packages, came to visit, stayed up late to welcome us when we came home, and got up early to see us off when we left. She would later become a devoted grandmother to my kids and nieces. And like I said, she never had another drink again. To me, the entire episode of her going away when I was seven—and of her ever drinking—quickly faded away, almost to the point of invisibility.

But my mother never forgot about it. Nor, as I later learned, could she put it out of her mind so easily. The day that Katie and I married, my mom pulled me aside at the beginning of the reception, before most of the guests had arrived. I could tell she was nervous, but I couldn't understand why. She then started talking about the best man's toast, and that there would be champagne. I wasn't following her and finally asked her, a little impatiently, what she was talking about. "I'm wondering," she said, "if it's okay with you if I have a sip of champagne after the toast."

I immediately said, "Of course, Mom, that would be great," and added, "You don't need to ask me. It's okay. Really. Don't even think about it. Okay?" I gave her a hug, but I could tell something wasn't right.

She quietly said, "Okay, thanks," but she didn't move.

And then I realized what she was really asking, which knocked the wind out of me. I looked back at her and said, "Mom, I forgive you." I explained that I wasn't sure I ever really blamed her, but if I did, I certainly had forgiven her a long time ago. I told her I was sorry she didn't know this already. And I tried to reassure her that everything she had done ever since was more than anyone could ever expect or want from a parent. A few hours later, we clinked glasses after the toast, but obviously, it wasn't the champagne that truly mattered.

What truly mattered was that my mother knew I forgave her. I am tempted to say that forgiving those you love—and letting them know that you forgive them—ought to truly matter to you. But I cannot say for sure, because what truly matters is up to you. My only suggestion is that you regularly ask this question—of others, for sure. But more importantly, you should ask this question of yourself, and you should answer it honestly and fearlessly. If you do, this question won't just help you get to the bottom of an issue or a problem. It will also help you get to the heart of your life.

CONCLUSION

The Bonus Question

I came across the bonus question recently while attending a memorial service for a very close friend and former law school roommate, Doug Kendall. As you might recall from Chapter Three, Doug is the lawyer who began the Constitutional Accountability Center by asking, essentially, "Couldn't we at least agree?" on a basic approach to interpreting the Constitution. Doug was a remarkably talented lawyer, a visionary leader, and an intensely devoted friend, father, and husband. He also had a special knack for asking great—you might even say essential—questions.

I first met Doug on a rugby field in 1989. We were both trying out for the Virginia rugby team. I remember Doug looking me up and down, but mostly looking down on me from his six-foot-four frame. He was massive, hence his nickname "The Big Man," and he had an extraordinarily large head with very thick brown hair, hence his alternative nickname, "Buffalo Head." Doug saw me and said, smiling, "Pretty small for a rugby player."

In the quarter century that followed, Doug and I became teammates, roommates, coauthors, and coconspirators. We didn't just play rugby together. We also went to the emergency room together (the two were connected). We once drank beer together from a dirty cleat (a charming rugby tradition); we biked, hiked, kayaked, and canoed; we traveled to Norway, Mexico, Costa Rica, Amsterdam, and California. We saw Bruce Springsteen shows and UVA basketball games. We obsessed over cowriting a long article on land use exactions—an obscure, but as Doug thought, *really important* topic; we coauthored op-eds about judicial nominations; we debated the original meaning of various clauses in the U.S. Constitution. There weren't many parts of my life that didn't intersect with Doug's.

Our other law school roommates were not a shy or retiring group. Yet even among this group of strong personalities, Doug was undeniably our leader.

He organized us, year after year, to get together. The tradition actually began in the spring of our first year in law school, in 1990, when Doug organized a trip to Watoga State Park in West Virginia. For the next twenty-five years, we continued to get together at least once a year, including our last gathering in Maine, a month before Doug died. Because of these gatherings, we became like family, like brothers, and it was all Doug's doing. He knew how important it was to get together, and he made sure it happened despite our increasingly complicated schedules, often by asking, "Couldn't we at least . . . ?"

Doug was not just our ring leader, he was also our cheerleader. He believed in his close friends and family more than we believed in ourselves. He never told us what to do, but he always asked how he could help. And help he did. He helped us become better versions of ourselves by asking us irresistible questions about our work, our relationships, our aspirations, and our fears—questions that provoked honest answers and, just like good keys, unlocked what we might have been hiding from others and ourselves.

Doug had a vaguely mystical quality to him. To be sure, the daily logistics of life often proved challenging for him. He didn't use the exact words "Wait, what?" but he asked a form of that question over and again. When we were in law school, for example, I would occasionally need a ride back to our house from Doug. We lived about ten miles away from the law school, out in the country on a small farm. When I would ask Doug what time he planned to head home, he often seemed flummoxed and would ask a version of "Wait, what?" And then he would suggest that I ask him again in a couple of hours. I would say: "*Ask* you in a couple of hours when you are going to go home? Not *meet* you in a couple of hours?" "Yeah," he would say, "ask me in a couple of hours."

I had an unfortunate habit of asking Doug just one question too many—old, annoying habits from the family dinner table are hard to break. When I crossed that line, Doug would go from being the sweet and gentle giant that he was into something quite different. We called these transformations "Doug-downs," because they were just like melt-downs, only bigger. So when Doug suggested I ask him about a ride home in a couple of hours, instead of acquiescing I would press him and ask him point-edly what he would know in a couple of hours that he didn't already know. He would reply along the lines of, "I'll know whether I want to drive your sorry ass home or make you walk ten miles. That's what I'll know." I would nod politely while taking a few steps back.

Yet even though Doug was often befuddled by the surface of life, I've never known someone more in touch with life's deeper currents. And for that reason, we all turned to him when we were mak-ing big decisions—about our careers, moving, or even whether to get married. Doug had a quiet way of sanctifying our decisions, not because he ever thought he had the power to bestow his blessing or that we should follow his advice, but because we all knew that Doug always kept his eye on what truly mattered. If what we were doing made sense to Doug, we were more confident that it was the right thing to do.

Part of what made Doug such a leader, both for his roommates and his colleagues, is that he was not cynical. He was abundantly sarcastic, for sure, but there was also a certain vulnerability to him, an open-ness. He was unafraid to show his passion for issues he cared about, even when they were obscure—like the Takings Clause of the Constitution, which Doug considered hugely important, even though you have probably never heard of it. Doug was never worried about seeming naïve, nor was he shy about expressing his genuine curiosity. He was never afraid, in other words, to ask "I wonder why?"

Doug died of colon cancer in 2016, at the age of fifty-one. On the back of the program for his memorial service was a poem by Raymond Carver, entitled "Late Fragment." The poem begins with what I am calling the bonus question, which is likely the most important question any of us will ever face:

> *"And did you get what you wanted from this life,
> even so?"*

The "even so" at the end of the question, to me, perfectly captures the reality that pain and disappointment are inevitably a part of a full life, but also the hope that life, *even so*, offers the possibility of joy and contentment. I suspect Carver, who was dying of cancer when he wrote the poem, was thinking of his own life, which had been filled with love and heartache, failure and redemption. For Doug's memorial service, the question reflected the bittersweet fact that Doug had lived a remarkable and wonderful life but had died far too young.

I cannot guarantee, of course, that if you simply ask the five essential questions in this book that you will be able to answer "I did" to the bonus question. But I do think the questions will help get you there, if you ask them regularly, because they can serve as a very useful guide to living a fulfilling life. After all, the questions cover a lot of important territory:

"Wait, what?" is at the root of all understanding.
"I wonder . . . ?" is at the heart of all curiosity.
"Couldn't we at least . . . ?" is the beginning of all progress.
"How can I help?" is at the base of all good relationships.
And "What truly matters?" helps get you to the heart of life.

If you live a life fueled by the ying and yang of curiosity and understanding; if you remain willing to try new things and to help and learn from others; and if you stay focused on what truly matters to you, I do believe you will be in a good position to say "I did" when it comes time to ask yourself the bonus question.

In suggesting that you think about what you want from life, I don't mean that you should take a selfish perspective or view life as solely something to take from rather than give back to. Nor am I suggesting that you should be thinking of material gain. I am simply suggesting that you consider now what will likely matter to you when your time has run out. My guess is that material gain will play a relatively small part in your final answer and that your relationships with others will be a crucial measure of your life.

This is, at least, how Raymond Carver viewed his own life. After asking: "And did you get what you wanted from this life, even so?" the poem continues:

I did.
And what did you want?
To call myself beloved, to feel myself
beloved on the earth.

The word *beloved* is important here because it means not just dearly loved, but also cherished and respected. Feeling beloved is not the sole measure of a life well lived. But I expect that for many of us, leaving this earth feeling loved, cherished, and respected is a worthwhile goal and, in the end, a worthwhile reward. Asking good questions—essential questions—and listening to the answers is as true a path as any toward this goal and reward. It is through such questions, after all, that bonds are formed and deepened.

My friend Doug showed as much during his life, which is why the Carver poem was so fitting for his memorial and why I have dedicated this book to his memory. Doug asked essential questions, and he listened carefully to our answers. He understood deeply the power, and beauty, of good questions. He was beloved by his family, friends, and colleagues, and he made all of us feel beloved in return. Indeed, Doug's life was proof that a sure way to feel beloved yourself is to help others feel the same.

And if you're not sure how to do that, just ask.

ACKNOWLEDGMENTS

This book would never have happened without Matt Weber, Meredith Lamont, and Miles Doyle, which means they are largely to blame. Matt and Meredith are truly remarkable and dear colleagues of mine at the Harvard Graduate School of Education, and it was their idea to post a short clip of my graduation speech online. I am certain it was the brevity of the clip, as much as anything else, that caused it to go viral and to come to the attention of Miles, an editor at HarperCollins. Miles gently but persistently encouraged me to turn the speech into a book, even after I expressed my belief that it wouldn't be possible given the demands of my day job and the fact that I wasn't sure I had anything more to say. Without his confidence and optimism, I would never have started the book, and without his deft editing and continued encouragement, I would never have finished it.

Several friends and family members read the manuscript, including Steve Gillon, Mimi Gurbst, Marcy Homer, Mike Klarman, Meredith Lamont, Daryl Levinson, and Matt Weber. They all offered great suggestions and, just as importantly, pretended to enjoy the stories. My wife, Katie, also read the manuscript and agreed—after I pleaded several times—not to delete the stories I told about her. She also helped me remember some old stories. Meanwhile, our kids—Will, Sam, Ben, and Phebe—generated some new stories while I was distracted writing this book, which I will share if there is ever a sequel.

Thanks also to my agent, Howard Yoon, for his expert guidance and assistance, and thanks to Progressive Publishing Services, who did a terrific job in copyediting the book. Thanks as well to my amazing assistant, Monica Shack, for helping me find time to work on this book.

The real joy in writing this book came from the opportunity it offered to reflect a bit on the friends and family with whom have I been blessed to share my life, and about whom many more stories could be told. To all of you, whether mentioned in these pages or part of stories that should never make their way into print, I offer my deepest gratitude and affection.